Sonic City

Making Rock Music and Urban Life in Singapore

Sonic City

Making Rock Music and Urban Life in Singapore

By Steve Ferzacca

NUS PRESS
SINGAPORE

© 2021 Steve Ferzacca

Published by:

NUS Press
National University of Singapore
AS3-01-02, 3 Arts Link
Singapore 117569

Fax: (65) 6774-0652
E-mail: nusbooks@nus.edu.sg
Website: http://nuspress.nus.edu.sg

ISBN 978-981-325-108-3 (paper)

National Library Board, Singapore Cataloguing in Publication Data

Name(s): Ferzacca, Steve, 1954-
Title: Sonic city : making rock music and urban life in Singapore / by Steve
    Ferzacca.
Description: Singapore : NUS Press, 2020. | Includes bibliographical references
    and index.
Identifier(s): OCN 1157333806 | ISBN 978-981-32-5108-3 (paperback)
Subject(s): LCSH: Rock music--Singapore--20th century. | Rock music--
    Singapore--21st century. | Rock musicians--Singapore. | Rock groups--
    Singapore.
Classification: DDC 781.66095957--dc23

Cover image: Artwork by Masonry Studios Pte. Ltd.

Typeset by: Ogma Solutions Pvt Ltd
Printed by: Ho Printing Singapore Pte Ltd

Dedication
For Tiger, Horse, Dog

虎
馬
狗

Contents

List of Figures

Acknowledgments

This all began with an appointment as a visiting senior research fellow with the Asia Research Institute (ARI) at the National University of Singapore (2011–2012). I was appointed as a member of the cultural studies cluster under the supervision of Professor Chua Beng Huat. Prof. Chua listened to the stories of my unfolding experiences in the Singapore music scene, and suggested I consider assembling my experiences as a kind of "project." While I was uncertain about moving forward with research that was and is so deeply personal, the stories I was hearing and the experiences I was having were compelling – especially as counter narratives, or at least other narratives that revealed absences in the official Singapore Story. With Prof. Chua's faith in the project (perhaps signified, at least for me, by his appearances at our performances), I proceeded. Without his faith and support this project would have never reached fruition.

Others at ARI contributed to this work in significant ways. Michael Douglass, head of the Asian Urbanisms cluster (to which I was assigned in 2016), afforded numerous opportunities to nurture and foster this work. Rita Padawangi and Michelle Miller were constant resources, listening and providing advice along the way. Tim Bunnell encouraged me to follow through, providing motivation to finish the book. I thank these colleagues for believing in this work, and showing up to many of our performances, talks, and other instances of musicking. Johnathan Rigg supported and encouraged this project from the beginning. Jane Jacobs (Stephen and Loli) by her very presence reminded me to attend in detail to the urban. Anjeline de Dios and Tejaswini Niranjana invited me to join a music and mobilities research group where we discussed many wonderful things.

Liew Kai Khun (KK) set the intellectual stage for all of this – he is a remarkable scholar, and I was blessed to have had the opportunity to meet and work with him. Lai Ah Eng, an ethnographer extraordinaire of the Singapore local kindly listened to my stories and explained some circumstances that I had misunderstood, gently offering insights that have been immeasurable all along the way. May Wang led us to her old neighborhood in Katong, and then joined me as I learned about Singapore. Allen Ziegler and the Kent Vale basketball crew kept me healthy. The Yale-NUS students who had to listen to many of these stories in the classroom were more patient than they needed to be – I am grateful for the opportunities to present to them this work.

Jamie Gillen was there from the very beginning. I can't begin to fully acknowledge the impact of his thoughts and comments as the fieldwork unfolded, and as the analysis and writing began. It was and is his friendship that has mattered most. Basketball, Kent Vale, listening to Tom Waits, dinners at Island Penang, consuming a little too much alcohol from time to time, Jamie was centrally involved and one reason why this time in Singapore was perhaps some of the best years of my life.

There are two from this motley crew of musicians, fans, and friends who appear in this book that have left a mark on my life and in my heart that will never disappear. Lim Kiang and James Tan introduced me to the worldings described in this book. Kiang and James leaned into me and invited me in – I can't believe my luck. As I've always said on stage, "I'm Steve Ferzacca, and these guys let me play with them." I also want to recognize the other members of The Straydogs – Ronnie, Jimmy, Jeffrey, Seow – who allowed me to become the youngest member of the band at 62. The Straydogs rehearsals and performances I was a part of were some of my most intense experiences in deep sound. The obligations and judgments involved deeply affected my fieldwork. Several childhood friends – especially Jeffrey and Shek – gifted me local histories of these youthful rockers.

And the gang – Victor, Noel, Clement, Allen, David, Kino, Bucci, Liu, Sally, Jeremy, Veron, Kenny, Sophie, Richard, the Lim family and so many more – thank you everyone in Singapore from the depths of my sonorous soul.

The people at NUS Press have been very good to me and wonderful to work with beginning with Pallavi Narayan who performed the initial review of the manuscript for the Press. When she described my book to me as a "friendly book," I knew then that this might all work out. Lindsay turned the volume down on my noisy text and tuned in on the harmonious moments. Finally, I am deeply grateful to Peter Schoppert and the support my project received from the Press.

Finally, without the support and love from the Ferzaccaberries – Jan Newberry and Ana Ferzacca – I could never have completed this project. A special shoutout to Ana for her wonderful photographs, some of which appear in this book. If you are interested in viewing some of our performances, search the internet for Blues 77, The Straydogs, Steve Ferzacca or Lim Kiang. We hope you enjoy these musical examples of sonic ethnography.

Foreword

Sonic City is a how-to guide for listening through reading. In bringing sound to story it can be described as a book about the poetics of music, told ethnographically. This book has refrains, stanzas, bridges, an outro, some intricate chord changes, and moments of transcendence. Reading this book you realize how unconventional it is because it is that rare academic book that oozes heart. The book looks back on the journeys of an academic sojourner by recounting the simple yet extraordinary process of what it means to take a stab at something – as an anthropologist, a musician, and a person. Ferzacca's storytelling is brave; there are a lot of mysteries about Singapore untangled in the book and these are as likely to be unknown to Singaporeans as to the rest of the global population. Yet this is not a tell-all but a matter-of-fact set of interleaved descriptions about how making music creates a city in the mold of one or two six-string electric guitars, a four-string bass guitar, drums, and vocals. As the book proves this is a much more difficult endeavor now than it was in the early days of Singaporean sovereignty but this does not stop the monograph's actors from daydreaming about a future where Dionysian dreams fueled by a 4/4 time signature return in full flower to the Little Red Dot.

What separates this tome from other ethnographies is its ability to move the traditional format of the ethnography forward through a multisensorial mixture of sound and sight, with taste, touch, and smell also making strong supporting appearances. If Stevie Wonder hadn't already taken the name as one of his records this monograph is like a Talking Book because it has the qualities of a singer narrating a period of his life on behalf of a group of people who like to talk a lot. Mostly these characters talk fondly about themselves and their role in Singapore's past, and speak less fondly about their unsettled place in Singapore's present. This is a sonic ethnography of music and of the value of the musical qualities of people's memories.

So maybe *Sonic City*'s second title should be called *Past Masters*, after the Beatles' collections of the same name. The musicians Ferzacca describes see in their past a more pure or authentic version of themselves, and in Singapore a country that used to be both more accommodating to their avant-garde lives and more impacted by their creativity. The path from juvenile mischievousness to adult conventionality to elderly afterthought mirrors so many lives caught in the buzz saw of the Singapore machine, which is always looking for better, faster, stronger… and younger. This is a classic ethnography in the sense that it shows (and does not tell) through sound what it is like to age in a city that has only token appreciation for the past and all the time in the world for the future.

Thus there is a sadness to the gentlemen in the book and it is not because they are older than most contemporary musical outfits or because they play a genre of music (blues) unknown to most of today's Singaporeans. Rather it is a sadness built out of a lifetime of secrets unveiled piece by piece by Ferzacca in sites as varied as WhatsApp messages and Ho Chi Minh City rock clubs and in venues as unique to Singapore as basement guitar shops and as common as Housing & Development Board (HDB) units. The sadness is clearest when the reader recognizes that the freewheeling attitude and creative energy of the musicians in *Sonic City* has been tempered over decades by the cultures of silence, fear, and anonymity that Singaporean society toils in.

There is another, more optimistic and joyful component to this book. This is an ethnographic exploration about a Singapore that is sonically exciting, versatile, and even joyful. It is one that travels, that morphs and distorts, that slobbers and barks, that forces you to put your stereotypes about the country and its people aside, to sit down and have a whiskey and listen to some music with it, to get on a plane with it and go somewhere like Yangon or Yogyakarta to enjoy some spontaneous revelry. *Sonic City* does an impressive job of encouraging the reader to think of a Southeast Asia for which Singapore is integral. The Singapore of *Sonic City* is one of conviviality, of smoking, drinking, and insouciance, and of undiluted performance and noise without purpose. This is the Singapore captured in Tom Waits' storyline:

We sail tonight for Singapore
We're all as mad as hatters here
I've fallen for a tawny moor
Took off to the land of nod
Drank with all the Chinamen
Walked the sewers of Paris
I danced along a colored wind
Dangled from a rope of sand
You must say goodbye to me.
– Tom Waits, "Singapore," *Rain Dogs*, 1985, Island Records

You are probably ready to listen to *Sonic City* by now, but allow me to share one last piece of musical reflection with you before you get on with it. Have you ever heard the album *A Love Supreme* by John Coltrane? It is an album made about the beauty of making human connection to a Higher Power. *Sonic City's* higher power is love generated through friendship and made supreme through music. Its stories revolve around Blues 77, the musical group featured throughout the book, and these could stand in for any group of non-biological sisters or brothers anywhere in the world who are bound together by a common interest and yet whose collectivity is not reduced to that singular feature. Friendship requires work, energy, and compromise, with the outcome being a string of individual notes that make up a song, which can make up an album, and which can make up a lifetime of friendship, like an oeuvre. Ferzacca's sonic ethnography is meant in two senses: the sonic ethnography that has notes, rhythm, tone, and tempo (the musicianship), and the one that illustrates the music of friendship. This is my favorite theme in the entire collection, the purest assemblage of them all, a glimpse of a group of people focused on the process of making friends with each other. This is the story in the book that really brings the noise for me. I hope that sounds like something you would like to listen to, too.

Jamie Gillen
University of Auckland
May 16, 2020

Overture

Deep Sound, Sonic Ethnography

Noisy People

It was around about midnight in Ho Chi Minh City. We were gathered on the rooftop of a high-rise overlooking Le Van Tam Park in the center of the city. I found myself there as a member of a Singaporean rock and blues band having a late night dinner with a group of Singaporeans after performing at a local Vietnamese bar that features live music. In fact, two Singaporean rock bands made the trip together, Khan Kontrol, a 1980s and '90s rock music cover band, and us, Blues 77, a blues rock band playing a mix of classic blues and original music.

Figure 1. Blues 77 performing at the RFC Club, Ho Chi Minh City, July 18, 2013. Photo by Thomas Ee.

During the performance, and up on top of the roof, I had to pinch myself to see if this was all really happening. There I was in this mythological place formerly known as Saigon that had haunted my life as a youth in so many ways – a faraway place I had never visited until as a 60-year-old anthropologist and bluesman. The late 1960s and early 1970s were defined, at least in my case, and for many of us growing up in the United States during America's Vietnam War, by this nation in pieces and this southern city. Television and newspaper images and stories were broadcast mostly from the south, and newsmen covering the war were mostly stationed in Saigon. Saigon provided a base of operations and a military restive place for R & R (rest and recreation). The city represented the destructiveness of conflict, the confluence of political histories and ambitions, but mostly for me, the perverseness of western arrogance. And so, my feelings post-performance on the rooftop oscillated from what the place had once meant to me, to a sense of amazement that accompanied the realization that this hippie-kid from the Midwest had just "played" blues music to an audience of Vietnamese in a legendary place, with some legendary Southeast Asian musicians.[1]

Lim Kiang, also known as Dennis Lim, "Old Man," and to all those who are core participants in this small community of musicians, family, friends, and fans, simply as Kiang, had arranged the "gigs." Kiang, at the time a 65-year-old bass player for Khan Kontrol, Blues 77 and The Machine (a Pink Floyd tribute band), as well as founder and bassist for a legendary 1960s Singapore rock band, The Straydogs (1966–1978), was working as a manager of a guitar shop when we met in the summer of 2011.[2] I arrived in Singapore that summer to take up a year-long appointment as a research fellow at the Asia Research Institute (ARI) at the National University of Singapore (NUS). I was assigned to the "cultural studies cluster" and intended to write a book of essays based on my ethnographic work in Yogyakarta, Indonesia, that began professionally in 1991. My assignment to the cultural studies cluster was determined by the nature of the book project: a culture writing exercise in which I was attempting to produce an ethnographic text that was not only structured by the way I learned about things in Yogyakarta, but also written under the influence of magical realism, a genre of writing that I thought best reflected my experience as an ethnographer during those years. I was trying to write the "marvelously real" (Carpentier 1949) for that was the way my experiences in Yogyakarta appeared to me, and I believe appeared to many of the Javanese and Indonesians I came to know along the way.

I traveled to Singapore for the appointment with my guitar, a hobby of mine since my teenaged years. Like many my age during the 1960s, music and sonic experience in general was a way we came to know our worlds and express ourselves in it – an "acoustemology" as Steven Feld (2012) describes in his ethnography of jazz musicians in Ghana. My sonic experiences in Singapore began almost immediately upon my arrival. In my first few days in Singapore, I located the guitar shops in town and on a Saturday afternoon made my way to the aging, bargain-priced Peninsula Shopping Centre where a number of music stores are located in the basement. I circled the guitar shops, entering most. As with all guitar shops, some stores in the basement were more inviting and user-friendly than others. Some store personnel are open to customer tryouts of gear, while other shops discourage it. Among the array of shops were music stores that sold mostly new equipment, carrying the major international brands, well known globally to all musicians and guitarists. I was pleased to encounter this familiarity and noted the presence of recognizable guitar gear that has always nurtured my own desires as a guitar gear consumer. Other shops dealt with used and vintage instruments only; a delightful surprise as I had not counted on finding such rare instruments in Southeast Asia. But one shop caught my eye – Guitar 77. Hanging in its display window was a 1990s Gibson Nighthawk sporting "pickups" that I was particularly interested in at the time. I walked in and asked the man behind the counter, a man about my age with long graying hair, if I could play the guitar.

"Sure," he said, and took it down from the display rack, found a cable, and hooked me up to an amplifier. I began playing licks and sections from a well-known blues song – "Stormy Monday."

"A blues man," the man announced. I smiled and commented on how much I liked the sound and playability of the guitar, and before long he retrieved an electric bass guitar from the display rack, hooked himself up and sat down with me to jam.

Kiang, the manager of the store who plugged me in, and I had barely spoken to each other. Instead, we established and continued our conversation through the combination of our amplified sounds in a sonic narrative, in this case the blues, a musical genre that we were both familiar with. In addition to making music together with our instruments I began to sing the lyrics, providing further structure to our sonic encounter.[3] After the "jam" ended I looked at Kiang, and said, "I know and you know we can play together." Not long after these early sonic experiences, James Tan, a 67-or-so-year-old self-made, successful businessman (a shipping container broker), and also the original drummer for The Straydogs joined Kiang and me to form Blues 77 – a blues rock (beats and blues) group performing original music and blues classics, incorporating along the way "young gun" Singaporean guitarists (Victor Chen, followed by Noel

Ong) and a blues harp player (Darrel Xin). And that was the beginning of our "play" that increased in intensity, commitment, and fun over the next four years and into the present.

This book is based on making music as a sonic element in a dynamic network of social relations that emerges as a small community of noisy people including amateur and semi-professional musicians, their families, friends, and fans. Since 2011, I have participated in this community as a musician and ethnographer, as a community member and researcher, as one more *ang mo* (Caucasian; lit. "red-haired") passing through Singapore, and as a friend. Over these years, I encountered and learned about a locally anchored "cosmopolitan commitment… yielding generously toward diversity" (Mignolo 2000: 269). This book documents the capacity to lean into difference and to localize "global designs" (ibid.). Localizing global designs involves reshaping the social within forms of exchange that emphasize principles of mutuality, that afford experiences of belonging, and, in this case, foster a sonic ethic, in place of the "subsistence ethic" Scott (1977: 2) describes for moral economies of peasant communities. Sonic obligations and exchanges dominate the sociality of this community. In addition to cosmopolitan conviviality and a sonic ethos, the gatherings of various kinds including happy hours and performances are often modalities for expressive masculinity. The cosmopolitanism celebrated in these pages is saturated in gender expressions and relations as well as to some degree in ethnic affiliation. The gendered soundscapes that form the infrastructure of this research are drenched in alcohol, male bonding, and English-language rock music. This urban ethnography reveals ways in which the city is sonically organized and produced. Spatio-sonic scales allow for "spaces of dependence and engagement" (Cox 1998) to exist dialectically as platforms for deep play and local politics. Modern sonic circuits along which music travels in the region, reflect regional histories and local judgments of taste. The "politics" involved in playing live music in Singapore, at the time of this fieldwork, was becoming increasingly entangled in the excavations of various types of heritage that have become national and civic past times in this Southeast Asian city. Our music community became caught up in these national designs in an attempt to revitalize the "swinging 60s" as valuable, noteworthy sonic ("intangible") heritage. From the neighborhood where Kiang and the others grew up, to a performance on a national stage, this book documents the somewhat accidental ascendance of a denigrated period of the Singapore Story to national recognition. The work here led to several conceptual frames I hope are useful: the notions of deep play and sonic ethnography. My involvement with this community afforded me the opportunity to understand Singapore in part as a sonic city where making rock music and urban life resonate as a way of knowing the world and participating in it.

The people I have come to know and play with over these years would be characterized by many Singaporeans as unconventional, atypical, noisy people. As one observer recently pointed out in the *Straits Times*, "noisy people" in Singapore need their own "playgrounds" (*Straits Times*, March 1, 2016: D5). I became involved over the years after that initial jam session in the aisles of a guitar shop with some noisy people in their own playgrounds: a guitar shop, a basement of an aging mall, several live music clubs, practice spaces and jam studios, performance venues, homes, hawker stalls, bars and pubs, in Singapore and around the region. All of these places are conducive to making noise; places for noisy people to participate in sonic experience that many describe as central to who they are as Singaporeans, but more so as participants in a cosmopolitan world. These sonic spatial practices are entirely urban, made with the preference for urban life. Such playgrounds and such noisy existence provide the possibility for participants to engage in what I refer to throughout this book as "deep sound."

Noise Pollution and the Urban Soundscape

Noise, and noisy people have been a concern in Singapore, becoming even more of a concern with independence (Low 2014). Lee Kuan Yew, Singapore's prime minister from 1959–1990, recognized as the "founding father" of this Southeast Asian nation state delivered a speech at a National Day Rally in 1986 where he outlined the necessary interventions the government had to legislate in order to achieve the goal of modernity. His attention to the social body is quite clear in his remarks:

> I am often accused of interfering in the private lives of citizens. Yes, if I did not, had I not done that, we wouldn't be here today. And I say without the slightest remorse, that we wouldn't be here, we would not have made economic progress, if we had not intervened on very personal matters—who your neighbour is, how you live, the noise you make, how you spit, or what language you use. We decide what is right. Never mind what the people think.

While Singapore's official discourse and legislation of the behavior of its citizens is deeply concerned about "noise pollution" and controling the sounds of its many different groups of people, I still found a sonic city filled up with noise and play.

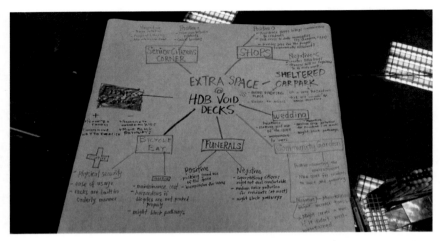

Figure 2. Whiteboard used during community meeting regarding sonic activities taking place in the void deck area. Photo by author, 2013.

The creative capacity under such circumstances is found wanting in some Singaporean circles. Singapore in its urge to be a high-ranking global city despairs in the low ranking it receives in the development of a creative class and industries compared to other cities. Richard Florida's (2002) arguments regarding the relationship between enhanced prosperity of cities that exhibit a dense, well-developed "creative class," has become a significant measure in the ranking of global cities. From this perspective, creativity involves the innovation and dynamism crucial to the life, livability, and ultimately prosperity of the city. Singapore ranks rather low on the creative index, and there has been concern in recent years that addressing this issue is of some importance if Singapore is to move up the global city scale.

A bit of history adds some irony to the recent concerns. The long-haired man I met at the guitar shop was in his youth a founding member of a popular 1960s rock group that recorded six singles for EMI Records before disbanding in the 1970s. In 1966, Kiang as a 16-year-old, took up the bass guitar with a band of brothers and friends all around the same age at a time when Singapore was emerging as a Southeast Asian nation state. The group known as The Straydogs was a part of a vibrant musical scene in Singapore and other cities throughout Southeast Asia. Kuala Lumpur and Penang, Malaysia; Saigon, Vietnam; Phnom Penh, Cambodia; Jakarta, Indonesia; and Bangkok, Thailand also had many local groups playing and recording English-language western rock and pop music.[4]

In Singapore and elsewhere in the region, this music making and other activities associated with it were denigrated by prevailing regimes. At the time of decolonization the provincializing of western values provided a moral compass for their citizenries and emerging societies. Ethno- and post-colonial nationalists feared the damaging influences of western popular culture on the peoples, and particularly the youth of these newly emerging nation-state societies. Bell-bottoms, miniskirts, and long hair were considered on the one hand to be "good clean fun" but on the other "subversive youth trends" reflecting the threatening and dangerous presence of "yellow culture." Likely a borrowing of concerns registered in response to the rise of American jazz and other popular music in the 1920s to 1940s Shanghai referred to as "yellow music" (Jones 2001), yellow culture in Singapore referenced not only a pornographic, obscene influence embodied in the "beat music of English-language bands" (Adil 2014: 136–137), but rather targeted a wide range of activities and expressive forms determined to introduce to the emerging nation state troubling western influences. Hong and Huang (2008: 87) report discussions of yellow culture taking place in the August 1960 legislative debates in which the Ministry of Culture identified the elimination of yellow culture as necessary to promote healthy cultural activities in Singapore. This led to crackdowns on cinemas, magazines, gambling, prostitution, jukeboxes, and secret societies, as well as music. The yellow culture campaigns of the late 1960s and early 1970s argued that traditional Asian values were being eroded by the westernization of an Eastern society. While local Southeast Asian bands playing the songs and sounds of popular music from Europe and North America "demonstrated" to local Southeast Asians that loving music was not only fun, but potentially an opportunity to be "creative and successful," the "hippism" associated with the music, the "unshaven facial hair, long hair, brawls that broke out at local performances led to youth harassment and banning of musical performances" (Thom 2014: 131; Adil 2014: 136).[5]

The People's Action Party (PAP) in the dawn of nation-building supported this stance against yellow culture (Tan 2003). "Cleaning up" newly independent Singapore (ibid. p. 407) meant cleansing away cultural matter considered out of place in an effort to restore a "distinctive" Singaporean culture "free of the 'westernization' eroding the 'traditional' values of Singapore's presumably 'Eastern' society" (Hong and Huang 2008: 87, 96).

Headlines from the years of the yellow culture campaigns indicate the wide range of images, activities, and associations that were of concern to the newly established government. The headlines that appeared in the *Straits Times* during the crackdowns tell a story and indicate a moral panic. For example in 1959 the "S'pore Govt. bans 18 pin-up magazines" (1959, June 7). In 1960 the government banned 65 publications not allowed to circulate in Singapore (1960, January 2). In addition to magazines in 1961 the government announced that films ("Now culture clean-up may move on films, warns minister" 1959, June 12), jukeboxes ("Culture clean-up hits jukes 1959, June 13), nightclubs ("Govt. closes eight clubs: 'They were used by gamblers'" 1959, August 14), and rock music aired over the radio waves were identified targets for cleansing. English-language rock music was denigrated for its association with the "hippy trail" (Police 'hit' the hippy trail and the message gets through 1970, April 4). Long hair was forbidden as it suggested the potential for rebellion (Long hair 'mark of a rebel' 1974, June 22). One of the ways to manage long hair was to require men with long hair to go to the back of the line ("Long hair means a long, long wait…" 1972, June 23), or to deny employment opportunities for persons with long hair ("Govt to bosses: Don't employ the long haired"1973, July 17).

It was during this era that Kiang and his brothers formed their band. Until the full impact of the crackdowns was felt, The Straydogs were able to perform and record. The band performed regularly for a few years at one of the tea dances in the Orchard Hotel in a club known as the Golden Venus. The band also played house parties, socials held at local military bases, and government venues like shows at the National Youth Council. Their presence in the community as a local rock band in the face of government-sponsored campaigns against this form of popular culture and entertainment was received both enthusiastically and with disdain. Much of the controversy surrounding the band was due to the fact that their sets included original music and covers of blues and blues rock songs, which the majority of Singaporean listeners were not familiar with. Nor could one dance to their music like the popular music performed by other bands on the scene that were mostly covers of familiar and danceable western pop songs. Singaporean audiences were attracted to a sonic worlding that featured English- and Malay-language musicking; for some a rude awakening begat by the 1961 performance of the British pop group, Cliff Richard & The Shadows. As Joe Pereira (1999) points out, the 1961 performance by The Shadows in Singapore at the former Happy Land Stadium had enormous impact on the history of popular music in Singapore. Singaporeans "covered" this "global pop" (Taylor 1997), which led to the pop music genre of "Pop Yeh-Yeh" (from the Beatle's 1963 hit "She Loves You [yeah, yeah, yeah]").[6] This youthful awakening, taking place at the same time as the national one, led to the establishment of "tea dances," and socials, national stages that formed the venues (spatio-sonic scales) for performances of popular music. These elements combined – making rock music during an era of government and public scrutiny, and continuing to make music in spite of negative audience response – have led to Kiang's and the band's legendary status in the local music scene until this day. In fact, these are the social historical facts that in the contemporary music scene and in the national imaginary that have come to cast this group of characters as worthy heritage material that can be referred to in a continuing revision of the Singapore Story.

Today government restraints and public demand (and scrutiny) remain in place shaping and shaped by the contemporary local configurations of art, performance, food and beverage, and entertainment. Such parameters are rarely mentioned as reasons for the inability of Singapore to nurture a creative class and economy. Censorship continues to have a strong presence, and familiarity in favor of originality from local bands remains. Real estate rates, licensing and zoning restrictions, and the haunting presence of the Public Entertainments Act continue to make life difficult for local artists to do much more than respond to public desire and government concerns; both formed to a great degree, but not entirely, by regional and global cultural industries. The concern regarding the development of cultural capital in Singapore is addressed at the government level by numerous grants and activities sponsored by the National Arts Council and private organization: grants meant to nurture the creative class. Kiang and the small community of musicians I have come to know are not generally considered appropriate members of this class, and so find themselves making music creatively without these incentives and supports. Yet recently, the troubled past of English-language rock music in Singapore has been rejuvenated as heritage. In the quest for cultural capital, bands and popular music from the 1960s and '70s once denigrated as yellow culture has found new space, however, always within arm's reach of government scrutiny, regulation, and control.

This book, then, examines the making of rock music in Singapore by a community of amateur and semi-professional musicians, their families, friends, and fans as simultaneously the making of urban life and vernacular history. This ethnographic rendition is derived from five years of fieldwork with this group of aging Singapore "heartlanders," "pioneers," and a diversity of others from various generations who congregate at a music store in a basement of a shopping mall located in the central business district in Singapore. The past and the present, embodied and experienced in the legendary status Kiang holds, as well as the legends of The Straydogs as underground, alternative popular music are organized in place-making among continually emergent, constantly in-the-making "associations of heterogeneous elements" of human and non-human "mediators and intermediaries" that entangle the connections of which Bruno

Latour (2005) terms "the social."⁷ This social work – the presence and emplacement of mediators and intermediaries participating in particular and a "peculiar movement of re-association and reassembling" – is performed and experienced to a great extent as the social of vernacular heritage (ibid. p. 7).

Before I continue following noisy people from playground to playground in Singapore and the surrounding region, I want to take a side trip to another Southeast Asian locale at a different time, where I first began thinking about sonic experience and the implications of understanding social relations in the resonance and reverberations that such activity produces. It was in a Javanese kampung in the city of Yogyakarta, Indonesia, that I began thinking about sound, soundscapes, and social life. It all began with a month's worth of rehearsals in the neighborhood where I was conducting fieldwork that brought a group of neighborhood men together to play a genre of Indonesian popular music known as *kroncong*. I want to return to these experiences as an example of what I refer to as deep sound. This brief side trip to Yogyakarta illustrates my approach to sonic ethnography and its possibilities for rendering social experience.

It's Not Just the Noise: Yogyakarta, Indonesia, 1992

After three days of lengthy negotiations (*tawar-menawar*) in the *ruang tamu* (front room of Javanese homes where guests are entertained) of newly made friends, surrounded by gamelan instruments, some complete, some awaiting final touches before beginning their travels around the world, I handed over the agreed upon rent (*kontrak*) for our home, and was given something to eat – of course. It struck me at the time that the presence of gamelan instruments "became a metaphor for the style of negotiations – refined, at least on the surface, tied together with strands of etiquette embodied in the language, action, gesture, body, space, and time" (field notes May 31, 1992) that was our conduct at the negotiation table (another metaphor).

Four brothers were negotiating on behalf of an older sister who, along with her husband, built and owned the house. The small house itself was new, and constructed within a very small space available in an already crowded compound. We were to learn more, later, about the implications of its presence as built form introduced into socially built lives (Newberry 2006). Not so unlike our own sudden import into the lives of our kampung friends and neighbors. Negotiations were in Javanese, a language I had no sense of at the time (and still don't), leaving my friend to broker negotiations on multiple levels. My field notes report "bursts of speech intermingled with excruciating lapses of silence, during which no one looked at each other, choosing to stare at the floor waiting for some tension to build towards speech." I go on to write "expressions were expressionless," and then I digress into lengthy descriptions (ever the dutiful anthropologist) of the conduct around drinking the sweet syrupy drinks that my friend's maid served us as we worked to come to an agreement on the year's rent for the house.

It wasn't until the end of the second day that a price was mentioned, at which time negotiations picked up at an amazing speed, and before I knew it we had arrived at a price for the year. The following day we discussed the details of the agreement (money to be handed over at a later time), at which time we were asked a series of questions that allowed myself, and my partner, to provide some background about who we were and what we were up to. The interchange had lightened dramatically, and smiles appeared in addition to idle chatting, questions about the instruments, and so on. During one of these lighter moments my friend's wife appeared in the doorway with their young daughter. She immediately dropped to her knees and entered the room, knee-walking her way to a place among us with her daughter in her arms. The visible social topography evoked spatial conduct to match, in this case, lowering one's body so as remain at the same level as those present in spatial terms, as we were all sitting on *tikar* (mats) arranged on the floor of the room. Several days later we met with the sister and her husband in the house itself, and handed over the cash, signing a rental agreement for the year.

Our arrival into the kampung (neighborhood) as we took up residence was met with a mix of curiosity, suspicion, ambivalence, and puzzlement, as well as some assumptions and expectations that we were unaware of at the time. Why have these foreigners (*orang asing*) decided to rent this house and live here? What will they do here? What will they eat? Will they shop here? What will this mean for our community? How will their presence matter?

This ambivalence and uncertainty were clearly expressed in the tentative approach displayed by our neighbors and others in the kampung in these early days of being there. The kampung children, of course, ignored this tentative sense of propriety, scampering in and out of our home, venturing into its deep recesses, for example the kitchen, where other older residents feared to tread. For those beyond the years of childhood, the face of the community towards our residence was standoffish and contemplating, waiting to see what our next move was going to be. The breakthrough came when my partner, also an anthropologist, began shopping for food in the local pasar to be cooked by her in our house. More importantly, or just as important, was the fact, made known

by the fearless children, that we ate nasi (rice) for breakfast. This social fact
sealed the deal and began our gradual integration into our corner of the larger
kampung community.

But as this aspect of social integration was taking place, and a relatively
gendered one at that, other aspects in this process were unfolding. My field
notes from these early days capture other (also gendered) aspects of the process
of social integration:

> From our perspective our only problem with our neighbours, well not
> our only problem, but one that is consistent is with the group of young
> men and boys who congregate nightly, daily, whatever, in front of our
> house. The bapak (lit. father, but household head) of the house next to
> ours built a small platform on stilts made of bamboo under a tree in
> the corner of our yard that connects to our front porch. The men and
> boys gather to play cards, chess, and sing and play guitars. The card
> playing and chess are quiet activities, but the guitar playing and singing
> are loud and go until 1:00 or 2:00 in the morning (night from their
> perspective). Their voices pierce our walls and I have already had many
> sleepless nights. (September 12, 1992, Yogyacarta, author's journal.
> pp. 102–103)

My notes go on to examine these activities in terms of local knowledge. As I
questioned some of my neighbors about the nightly crooning, it was explained
to me that these young men had little to do (*malas*). It is important here to
consider this explanation briefly. *Malas*, the term used by our neighbors, is
often translated into English as "lazy." Unfortunately there is a burden of
cultural baggage carried in this translation, especially an emphasis on the will
and agency of individuals and groups that hearkens colonial imagery and
attitudes of the lazy native. But my understanding of the intent of this term as
it is often used by my neighbors is as an observation of individuals in context in
which action is required, but more so with an emphasis on whether or not
context provides possibilities and limits for action to occur. I have described this
structure of and for experience elsewhere (Ferzacca 2001), drawing upon other
anthropological descriptions of the kinds of contexts for action that appear in
Javanese expressive culture. Javanese experience, and especially in the case of
working-class Javanese for whom life's choices are engaged within class-based
constraints, is organized within a labyrinth of forces, energies, spirits, bodily
winds and fluids, and, of course, people and things that make up the social life
of the Javanese.

This phenomenologically apparent labyrinth forms a complex of limits,
possibilities, and coincidences in the production and reproduction of Javanese
subjectivity, what I refer to as the pneumatic self (drawing upon Coomswarmy's

[1977] cultural psychology described from another context). This labyrinth, experienced as copious flows and pneumatic winds, saturates human existence, emphasizing a notion of experience (*pangalaman*) that takes shape within desire for a fluid fitness among a complex of coincidently aligned and dynamically interdependent categories of power and elements within the universe (Ferzacca 2001: 19). Such a cultural logic has some deep roots and certainly some primordial illusions attached, but, nevertheless, represents an adaptation anchored in the confluence of a ranked society, colonial, post-colonial, and class-based consciousness and practicalities. *Malas*, then, is hardly an individual personality (or group) characteristic, neither is it a psychological predilection, although these explanations are available. Rather, *malas* is a context in which possibilities for action are absent or not required. I was told that the majority of this particular local group of young men – the late night crooners – were without responsibilities; at the moment they had no jobs, no wives, no children, and therefore no need to attend too much of anything that typically happens in the morning.

In an earlier analysis of the events associated with music in the kampung (Ferzacca 2006) I focused on the local political economy of gender relations with a non-local analytic category of "musicking" in order to understand the appearance and then disappearance of the *kroncong* music rehearsals. What I did not do was locate a specific observation of musicking in the intra-sonics of community-based musicking, or in kampung sonority sounded-at-large. In the earlier analysis I did not include the late-night crooners. The making of *kroncong* music must be understood within the intra-sonics of community-based musicking that, as deep sound, remains situated in the soundscape of the kampung community, which for me began with the "rough music" (Thompson 1993) described at the outset.

This noise was most certainly, at least in part, directed at us. The late-night crooning was a musicking of kampung social relations, a making of social relations, and an appraisal of local affairs. Christopher Small (1998) describes musicking as musical "activity by means of which we bring into existence a set of relationships that model the relationships of our world, not as they are but as we would wish them to be." Alfred Schutz (1964) similarly describes making music as making social relations, however, with less attention on the norms and ideals that musical performances necessarily draw from. It was a musicking similar to the "rough music" Thompson addresses in the European context in which music is public culture used to comment upon local realities and, in particular, instances in which community members were judged to have been involved in "crossing forbidden frontiers or mixing alien categories" (Thompson 1993: 509). The late night rough music made me aware of a "mode of life in which some part of the law belongs still to the community and is theirs to enforce" (ibid. p. 530). What I felt as noise, was noise for me. My exchange with this music evoked my valuation of it as noise that also evoked "ideas of the causes that produce it, dispositions of action, reflexes" (Nancy 2007: 15) indicative of the centrality of exchange in sensing sound or sensing in general. This musicking within a ""the whole system of sound" (ibid.) centered on the local function of making music as a cultural mode, a performativity used to judge, comment, appraise the dynamic conditions of social relations in the kampung: a project I want to refer to as deep sound.

Deep Sound

What do I mean by deep? I follow Geertz, Huizinga, and others here. In Geertz's (1973) analysis of the Balinese cockfight, he notes that as the attention of the participants is drawn to the betting at the center of the cockfight ring rather than the betting taking place "outside," the deepening of the play begins. The play becomes deep because the attention has deepened and shifted, due to the quantity and quality of the bets – or perhaps more precisely, the quality and quantity of exchanges – for which interest shifts from attention to whether or not a particular rooster will win or lose to the relative human status transacted through exchange, and not only the cockfight itself. Geertz argued that what becomes "at stake" in such circumstances is framed by a local and particular moral economy, in this case among Balinese men, in which esteem, honour, dignity, and respect are emergent and relative to the cockfight itself. As Kleinman et al (2011) note, deep is the moral system itself, shifting to reflect history, predictable yet as highly variable as our persons and their histories. "Deep" in my usage highlights the capacity of sound to circulate and so provoke attention to moral life in the kampung as a "device of saturation" (Foucault 2007). As sound (and noise) "spreads in space" so does the capacity of sound to connect, to share, and therefore evoke contact, and so "participation" (Nancy 2007: 10). This is what I mean by deep sound.

Sonic participations, such as those late-night songs on the doorstep to my house are subject positions in a soundscape, in this case the soundscape of Indonesian kampung life, performed and heard as an "audible dialogue with the world" (Hirschkind 2006: 83). Such resounding forms of agency reflect as many ways and as many perspectives as there are kampung residents. One channel from which to enjoy the kampung soundscape is to listen to its sonority as a resounding of the moral economy of kampung existence – it is everyday politics and operates somaphorically (Ferzacca 2010) as one of among several "visceral modes of appraisal" (Connolly 1999) available to kampung residents. A somaphore, in my formulation, denotes the body (soma) as an ongoing bearer of lived experience, and so the carrier (phore) of all sorts of meaning, affective and otherwise. Unlike the approaches of Lakoff and Johnson (1980) that note the importance of the body in creating consciousness with and through embodied metaphors, or language, I propose that the body is consciousness, therefore, the body (soma) is an ongoing bearer, and so carrier (phore) of meaning. Perception, movement, and physical experience somaphorically link the domains of body, subjectivity, and society respectively. Somaphoric organizations of society refers to the manner in which individual or social experiences of social positions, statuses, roles, tasks, obligations, and derivations from such subject positions of men, women, old and young, haves and have-nots, and numerous other subject positions in this case and in the following are audible as the noise of daily life. Rather, what we have is the everyday audible dialogue of social structure and praxis.

Take for example, the daily street cleaning performed by kampung residents. The stiff bristles of the broom swish across the narrow street and alleyways as every afternoon kampung neighbors clean in front of their homes in preparation for *sore*, the late afternoon–early evening social time that takes place in kampung all over Yogyakarta, and Java for that matter. The broom sounds the time but also the fulfillment of social obligation and contract expected of neighborly participation in the daily life of the community. Throughout Indonesia community cleanliness is a government dictum as well as a locally sanctioned value. The acronym Bestari – *bersih* (cleanliness), *sehat* (healthy), *tertib* (orderly), *aman* (safe), *rapi* (neat), and *indah* (beautiful) – represents the government interest in such things, but in the corners of kampung like ours it's governance that matters as much if not more so. The sound of the broom is a call to others that the time has come to act as members of the community. As decades of ethnography have illustrated, for Javanese, whether living in the *desa* and *dusun* (villages) of the countryside, or the urban villages like the kampung we moved into, "living publicly" (Mulder 1992: 41) is a paramount feature of everyday life. Patrick Guinness (2009) reviews once again the literature on Javanese kampung life and the emphasis on "social harmony" (*rukun*) in and for community life. What still matters, in the past, and in the more recent present is proximity to *tetangga* (neighbors) on one's left and right (*tetangga kanan-kiri*) in terms of simply getting along on a daily basis. This getting along with one's immediate neighbors is managed by fulfilling daily duties and obligations, like sweeping the street and splashing water on it afterwards to settle the dust in front of one's house; this is done each day at the same time by residents, or the maid if the household has one. The sound of the coconut stick broom (*sapu*; *gagang sapu*) resounds with such depth; it is deep sound because it is a sound of reciprocal exchange, embedded in and embodied by numerous other daily exchanges that signal social participation, or at least the willingness (or unwillingness) to participate in social life.

Sweeping the alleyway in front of one's home before *sore* begins brings about attention, and, so, is the "sensuous conduct" (Crossley 1998) Javanese who live in this urban kampung value. Such everyday and daily sensuous conduct is one source from which to appraise the competence of others, and operates as I have argued elsewhere as the somaphoric organization of social life. The materiality from this perspective of the somaphor is sounded, deeply, as the sonority of everyday kampung life, a resounding presence of human and non-human forces immersed within labyrinths of interaction and anticipatory exchange among actual social relationships in salient, actualized works of the imagination.

Deep sound resounds profoundly – it is soundings from the fathoms of social life. The profound implications and consequences of deep sound are multi-sonorous in affect and meaning, the depth enabled by the milieu in which social lives occur. Foucault (2007) described the milieu as "a certain number of combined, overall effects bearing on all who live in it" (p. 21). This immersion opens up participants experientially to local "devices of saturation" (ibid. p. 45) that are points and moments of "intensification" in local experience. Saturation is a common Javanese theme as well. Geertz (1960: 238) wrote that an "articulate informant" explained that "feeling" and "meaning" is life. This Javanese phenomenology is captured by the concept of *rasa*, which Geertz's informant described as "whatever lives has rasa, and whatever has rasa lives" (ibid.). Geertz elaborated further on *rasa*, and others (Stange 1984), including myself, have worked this concept over as well. There are two points I want to emphasize here. First as Geertz (1960) pointed out, Javanese tend to view subjectivity from this phenomenological analytical perspective in which "feeling" and "meaning" are one and "tied to everything." Secondly, this "everything" is the crux in terms of being a person the Javanese way. As a particularly articulate informant related to me in 1992, some 30-plus years after Geertz, the lived everything matters:

> Tap the copious flows that saturate your authentic identity. The meaning of this is rasa lives. We feel because we live, and life saturates our entire body. (Galilah rasa yang meliputi seluruh tubuhmu, kepribadianmu yang asli. Artinya, rasa itu hidup. Kita bisa terasa ini karena kita hidup. Dan hidup itu meliputi seluruh tubuh.) Malang, Indonesia (East Java), June 24, 1992.

This fundamental feature of Javanese experience (*pangalaman*) that is conceptualized as saturation in life, a life characterized as feeling and meaning (*rasa*) as one, provides an entry into making sense of society in Java. In order to understand the manner in which Javanese direct us to the centrality of somaphoric organizations, this sense of self is crucial to consider (see Ferzacca 2001). In this way the content of daily life is felt content. The sounds of the broom that are audible each day resound as a device of saturation, compelling as "surveillance procedures" but more importantly, as a call to the human feeling of community.

The social fabric of kampung experience is not only rendered but is validated in sensuous terms. Deep sound captures this attention to the everyday exchanges that make up individual experience and social existence in such communities. Sound as Nancy argues is "made of referrals" (Nancy 2007: 7). As sound spreads in space "meaning and sound" come to share "the space of the self, a subject" (ibid. p. 8). Sound-meaning, then, resounds in places by "resounding in me" (ibid.). Nancy (ibid. p. 10) goes on to say that this echoing is accomplished through the "methexic" (Huizinga's methectic) qualities of sound that capture human attentions, resonating "participatory" experience as a contagious form of exchange – "sharing." Sound as sense, to summarize these points Nancy makes perhaps too briefly, "is the ricochet, the repercussion, the reverberation: the echo in a given body" (ibid. p. 40). James Donald notes John Cage and his distinction between silence and sound "not so much acoustic as a question of attention" (2011: 34).

The rough music performed upon our arrival should be heard – listened to – as "populist ideology," (Fox 2004) that expresses and codes "class specific cultural response(s)." Considering Fox and Thompson in light of my earlier analysis brings special attention to a tradition of popular culture studies that view expressive cultural practice often from below for its "social and cultural contradictions... fracture and oppositions within the whole" (Thompson 1993), "mediated primarily by ritualized forms of intimate social interaction" (Fox 2004: 30). Rough music is a "working class art" (ibid. p. 31), in that its making on those cool evening in a central Javanese city expressed, captured, absorbed, penetrated, administered within the "simple jurisdiction" (Nancy 2007: 52) the intimate social interactions that make up in the social lives and arrangements in this corner of the world. Rough music, then, is a tactical and strategic capacity of making sense. In this way, the rough music as deep sound requires engagements in the daily exchanges that saturate the experiences of local milieu. The rough music richly expressed local notions of self and person, economies of gender relations, the felt content of moral life among neighbors, and the entry of alien categories in a deeply rooted milieu. The sonic depth of rough music then lives among the somaphoric organizations of everyday life.

Sonic Ethnography

Aural and sonic histories, sounded anthropologies and documented acoustemologies are becoming more common.[8] As described above, I ventured into this realm of research and analysis prior to my arrival in Singapore. Based upon musical experiences in another place, I centered on the proposal that making music was an attempt on the part of some men in an Indonesian kampung to address their increasing impotence as men in the affairs of kampung life. The country and rustic elements of *kroncong* music in that case, as well as the unbridled masculinity sometimes associated with some *kroncong* musicians were re-assembled as a locally meaningful ensemble or sonorific structuration that introduced into the kampung soundscape a novel yet familiar phonography of social life. In that article I explained that in the making of *kroncong*, as Huizinga noted (1950: 14) both "methectic and mimetic qualities" are at "play" – the sonic action involving the kampung relevant social of the music performed augmented by the sensibila and musicality of *kroncong* music's "sound of sound" (ibid.) is similar to the double layering of "sentience and copying" Taussig (1993: 80) refers to emergent in processes of cultural appropriation. The sonic depth here is about correspondences and consequences rather than merely acoustics, or the recognitions of signs. Attempts to appropriate the social attentions of kampung residents (along with myself) as I described them illustrate the ways in which I imagine sound is deepened (Ferzacca 2012).

This ethnographic project emerged from my hobby, from the habits of my personal life, and not from an officially funded research project with grant in hand. As my experiences with this small community of musicians mounted into something regular, I became aware that I was learning about Singapore as a researcher just the same. The stories I told my academic colleagues at the research institute and at the National University of Singapore were met with great interest, followed by, "Are you going to write about this?" At some point I decided I needed to talk to my new musician friends about whether or not they were interested in becoming collaborators, interlocutors involved in anthropological research that would illustrate and tell their stories as their stories had entered mine. Kiang, James, and the others were enthusiastic, and encouraged me to continue.

I am now referring to this work as sonic ethnography. Sonic ethnography takes seriously the notion that sonic participations are "sonic knowledges" in the making (Smith 2000). Frith remarks that, "making music isn't a way of expressing ideas; it is a way of living them" (1996: 111). One possibility for subject positions and subjectivities to a greater or lesser degree resound in social soundscapes, and so can actualize as sonic expressions of social prowess and assemblages of the social in an audible sociology. The methods of sonic ethnography are the same for any ethnographic enterprise: participant-observation, interview, and long-term fieldwork. I have been involved with this community on and off for six years as an anthropologist and as a member of several Singaporean rock bands. Participant-observation and interview have been key approaches, but also the degree of "participant-experience" (Pink 2009) as a band member has been intense and deep. This sonic ethnography has taken me around Singapore and Southeast Asia. We've toured as a band performing in Melaka and Ho Chi Minh City. We've also traveled to Yangon, to check in on guitar shop operations.

In addition to this performance aspect of this ethnographic encounter, we write songs about everyday life in Singapore that are conscious attempts at actualizing representation in ethnographic performance – an example of a "modality" in addition to the use of text and image in articles, books, blogs, and so forth. For example, an original composition that Blues 77 has become known for is "Shiok-lah." The song is not based on the etymology of the word "shiok" (Malay), but riffs off the use of shiok and its exuberant rendition, shiok-lah, in Singapore. One late morning while I was waiting for Kiang to show up at the shop, a clerk asked me if I had tried the kaya toast set at Kopitiam in the Funan Mall next door. I said I had not to which he replied, "You should, it's shiok man. Coffee, two eggs with kaya toast, *shiok-lah*!" I immediately left for the coffee shop, ordered myself a kaya toast set and began writing the song. By the time Kiang showed up, I had the basic idea and talked it out with him. Later in the evening I wrote the music and brought the song to the shop for Kiang, James, and I to play. Here are the lyrics:

"Shiok-Lah" (Key of A)
She puts kaya on my toast, milk and sugar in my tea.
She puts kaya on my toast, milk and sugar in my tea.
Two eggs in a saucer – shiok-lah – that's all I need.
Then she crawls under the covers – shiok-lah – come on take care of me.
She turns water into wine, salt and flour into mee.
She turns water into wine, salt and flour into mee.
Two eggs in a saucer – shiok-lah – that's all I need.
When I come home late, she's there waiting for me.
She puts bourbon in my coffee, she brings home chicken rice just for me.

She puts whiskey in my kopi, makes chicken rice just for me.
Two eggs in a saucer – shiok-lah – that's all I need.
Then she crawls under the covers, come on take care of me.
Take care of me, take care of me, take care of me.
(Ferzacca 2012)

The first performance of the song in a small club in Chinatown made us acutely aware that perhaps this one was a keeper.[9] But more importantly, composing and performing the song provided insight into possibility, and a way to express ourselves collaboratively, perhaps somaphorically. We consciously included the sexual euphemisms common to blues music (She puts kaya on my toast…). We consciously selected a blues riff that "imitated" those composed by the African-American blues players influencing our music – Muddy Waters in this case. These sonics fused with "shiok" represented, actualized, and performed the values that brought us together as a group, and, as I contend in this book inform the making of this small community as well – cosmopolitan conviviality – a cosmopolitan feasting was what we were after. The music we composed surrounded events and experiences of the day that affected us in some way. We wrote about medical events that took place during a jam session (hey, we're old, things happen)[10], cyclones in The Philippines,[11] being lonely with no one to telephone,[12] shopping with our wives,[13] a trip to Yangon, Myanmar,[14] being in love with someone,[15] spontaneous moments of insanity.[16] And while we based most of our music on shared experiences, it was clear because of our particular histories we "shared experiences" differently. For example, the Ho Chi Minh City experience for me was historically charged in a particular way. The Chinese owner of the restaurant at some point in the evening brought out a guitar along with scotch and whiskey. Some of us played a tune or two but when Kiang picked up the guitar and began to play, I became aware of how different a shared experience can be for each person. My first visit to this town as a performer and as a member of the entourage from Singapore was heightened by the fact that I had spent a great deal of my youth protesting America's Vietnam War. My academic performance in school was affected by my loyalties to the cause, my social relationships determined, my adolescent and young-adult sensual life framed by my social imaginary at the time. So, sitting on top of the world in Ho Chi Minh City over 40 years later in these circumstances stunned me, and continued to stun me as we sang "Ohio" by Crosby, Stills, Nash, and Young, and "Blowing in the Wind" by Bob Dylan, and on and on.[17]

But as Kiang sang "Route 66" I came to realize that "Saigon" meant something else to Kiang and the others entirely (discussed further in Chapter 4).

For young Kiang, the Dennis Lim of the early Straydogs, Saigon was a musical opportunity but also a place, like Singapore, where one could engage a cosmopolitanism that was also a gateway to global modernity. For an aging Kiang, Ho Chi Minh City is a source of musical opportunity, cheap entertainment, and recreation. It reminds him and others of an earlier Singapore, the on they grew up in, before the sanitation that has taken place over the course of their lifetime. When Kiang was young, his father, The Chief, believed Saigon was a den of debauchery and drug use, and he forbade his son from performing there in fear of him becoming a heroin addict. His father would be turning in his grave, perhaps, if he knew about his aging son's escapades in this "R & R" city.

I also include in my data the music community's use of social media and instant messaging (Facebook and WhatsApp), as well as the many audio and video recordings we have made of our performances and rehearsals. Historical documents from the National Archives of Singapore Oral Histories Project were consulted, along with various other media, newspapers, recordings, and video available from a variety of sources.

For the most part, this sonic ethnography is a study of popular culture as signifying practices rooted in the everyday routines and habits of contemporary life in Singapore. I see the making of rock music among the members of this community as central to the making of social order, the transformation of consciousness, and forms of social action in a "struggle for the city" (Harvey 1985). The "cultural producers" (Mahon 2000) that appear in these pages produce aesthetic dispositions, cultural values, ideologies, and identities, and they do so within the constraints of urban life in the city state. In this milieu, making rock music is an experience and performance that intensifies local social relations revealing the productive and resistant nature of power. While the city and the government provide "spaces of dependence" (Cox 1998) that inflict institutional, sociological, and historical constraints, the manner in which these spaces are used by this community of musicians generates "spaces of engagement" (ibid.) that allow for the expression of history, identity, and the social that is meaningful in an intensely local way of knowing the world to which sound is central. The randomly produced jingle-jangle noise encountered in the basement of the Peninsula Shopping Centre located in the heart of Singapore's business district, especially on weekends, hardly seems to be the kind of deep sound that offers insights into the social. Little did I know what was in store for me.

Chapter One

Crossroads

If you want to learn how to make songs yourself, you take your guitar and you go to where the road crosses that way, where a crossroads is. Get there, be sure to get there just a little 'fore 12 that night so you know you'll be there. You have your guitar and be playing a piece there by yourself... A big black man will walk up there and take your guitar and he'll tune it. And then he'll play a piece and hand it back to you. That's the way I learned to play anything I want.[18]

Figure 3. The Peninsula Shopping Centre, Coleman Street entrance. Photo by author, 2012.

Cosmopolitanism and the Social in a Southeast Asian Place

Crossroads is a reference to Singapore as S Rajaratnam's (1972) "Global City."
A city he said "is the child of modern technology. It is the city that electronic
communications, supersonic planes, giant tankers and modern economic and
industrial organization have made inevitable" (ibid. p. 225). A city linked
"through the tentacles of technology" to a "world-wide system" (ibid. p. 226).
A "global port" that "makes the world its hinterland" (ibid. p. 227). As a global
port Singapore has drawn people from all over the region and world, some
passing through, and some who have remained on this small island located at a
crossroads in the Asian maritime trade network. Crossroads also refers to the
guitar shops located in the basement of the Peninsula and Excelsior Shopping
Centres located on Coleman Street in Singapore's downtown central business
district. And crossroads also refers to the cultural and social exchanges that I
have observed taking place in this sonic city. But perhaps most importantly,
crossroads is a musical reference well known to rock and blues musicians. In
this chapter, the character of the community and its vernacular heritage centered
on cosmopolitan conviviality is developed in both the literal and figurative
sense of the crossroads.

It seems for all people at all times, crossroads are a place marked in some way
as special among human places. Crossroads (or crossways) are found in Vedic
literature, Pali texts, Chinese medical treatises and hagiography, as well as
Southeast Asian tales and histories, and are described as places where "meritorious
public works" (for example the building of stupas) can occur alongside the
public flogging of criminals. The Buddha and Buddhists erect stupas at
crossroads (Kosambi 1962). In Vedic literature crossroads were homes to
Mother-Goddesses ("Mothers-companions"), who because of their ability to
speak different languages offered wanderers opportunities for domestic offerings
to be made to family deities and ancestors, therefore localizing a stranger's
experience (ibid.). At the confluences of human movement that include but are
not limited to roads and waterways, people often encountered "great
harmonizers," gate-watchers, keepers, teachers, monks in contemplation,
"guardians of the boundaries," devils, and other harmful entities.[19] Attention is
paid to crossroads and crossways because of this potential. And so such places,
in the classic and modern sense, are often located at the outskirts of sedentary
human settlement, are envisioned and experienced as inauspicious places where
goddesses, devils, enchanters, guides, gift givers carry on as human movements
activate their presence. While crossroads are artifacts and perhaps even maps of
and for human movements, crossroads and crossways are always local sites
"made to do something" among the emergent connections that not only haunt
but make up these places (Latour 2005: 191).

For musicians and connoisseurs of American blues music, the crossroads refers to a mythic tale of a Faustian bargain. As the story goes, the father of blues music, Robert Johnson, received the ability to play the blues on his guitar after selling his soul to the devil at the crossroads. In fact, the story should be attributed to a blues player also from the early 20th century, Tommy Johnson, who, when interviewed, provided the basic gist of the story. The devil, in Tommy Johnson's rendition, is a teacher who Tommy "jams" with as he learned to play the blues on his guitar. While this storied version of the crossroads reflects African and African-American histories and sensibilities, many features of the crossroads found elsewhere around the world appear. In 1936, Robert Johnson recorded "Crossroad Blues" which is not a story of a Faustian bargain, but rather begins with a verse that has someone kneeling in despair begging forgiveness, followed by an anxious verse as failed attempts to hitch a ride evoke resignation and fear with nightfall approaching. "Crossroads Blues" reveals the potential of the crossroads to harmonize and vex human lives.

> "Crossroad Blues" by Robert Johnson
> Recording of November 27, 1936
> San Antonio, Texas
> I went to the crossroad, fell down on my knees
> I went to the crossroad, fell down on my knees
> Asked the Lord above, "Have mercy, save poor Bob, if you please"
> Mmmm, standin' at the crossroad, I tried to flag a ride
> Standin' at the crossroad, I tried to flag a ride
> Didn't nobody seem to know me, everybody pass me by
> Mmmm, the sun goin' down, boy, dark gon' catch me here
> Oooo, eeee, boy, dark gon' catch me here
> I haven't got no lovin' sweet woman that love and feel my care
> You can run, you can run, tell my friend-boy Willie Brown
> You can run, tell my friend-boy Willie Brown
> Lord I'm standin' at the crossroad, babe, I believe I'm sinkin' down.

It is at a crossroads where this project began, and of course it is at a crossroads where this project remains. In this chapter I explore a local place in Singapore that itself has been commonly characterized as a "crossroads to the East." The sonic experiences that I explore in this book are situated in an urban cosmopolitanism that is the history and historicity of modern Singapore, both as a colony and city state. From "Straits Settlement" to "Global City" Singapore is the meeting place of numerous ethnic groups who came to the island to seek prosperity. This plural society was rationalized during the colonial period into a rubric that includes Chinese, Malay, Indians, Eurasians, and Others, referred to by the acronym CMIEO (Siddique 1989), that continues today. The Malay ethnic group is the only ethnic group indigenous to the island. All of the other ethnic groups and nationalities, including those glossed over by the "other" category (everyone outside the other four classifications) are imports. "Foreign talent" attracted to this crossroads of the East that became the hub of the Asian Maritime Trade Network after its establishment as a station of Britain's East India Company in 1819 included diverse groups attached to numerous networks of trade in Asia and the world. The longue durée of this island trading port city is its location along trade routes connected by waters, straits, surrounding seas and oceans (Guan, Heng, and Yong 2009). Singapore's pluriverse community reflected its location along the Straits of Melaka as a shipping lane and fluid trade route linking the Indian Ocean to the South China Sea. As a crossroads of trade and commerce, Singapore has always been cosmopolitan. Cosmopolitanism is its nature and its history.

Encounter and Discovery: Singapore, October 30, 2011

I arrived in Singapore on September 1. I had been invited to a dinner and passed a small mosque (mesjid) along the way. A muffled call for prayer seemed less like a sound system with the mute turned on than a resounding of Koranic Arabic turned inward on itself. A week later the cityscape around Raffles City Mall was turned into a Formula One racetrack for the highly anticipated weekend race. Formula One racing cars make a great deal of noise. Several dozen of these machines screaming around the city produced a roar that could be heard well beyond the fences covered with tarpaulin that had been constructed around the city circuit. The *Straits Times* published many stories prior to, during, and after the race. One story noted the social qualities of the scream of the track as "sexy, successful."[20] The majority of the *Straits Times* articles that appeared after the September 25 race pondered the appropriateness of formula racing in Singapore because of the noise.

The muted voice of the mesjid is perhaps the subject of an "urban utopia," sonic rationality, properly resonant in and for the modern city in which respect for the "privacy of the citizen" reflects the engineering and management of civil society so to speak. This muted human activity abates the possibility of cultural and social disintegration.[21] The scream of racing car engines is equally modern, roaring the heavy metal of technological advancement. The power chords of the racing car roar to remind everyone who can hear it of Singapore's amazing history of development: always a cyborg-nation of machine, human sense, and skill, at high velocity through space and in time.

Searching for an anchor, a familiarity I could use to settle my arrival anxiety, I headed for some guitar shops I had located using online searches before leaving my prairie home. I had been to Singapore before, and so knew enough to buy a transport pass for use on the trains and buses that network this small island city. Taking nothing with me except a pocketful of guitar picks, I headed "downtown" – a locater that is entirely my own. Arising from the subterranean chute of screech and halt, through which moving masses of hand-held device holding locals and "others" assemble and flow, the sun and heat greet me without compromise – at least today.

Take it slow, I say to myself as I walk, knowing that I sweat easily, which, added to the unease of new encounters, leaves me dripping, drenched, and sloppy. A whitewashed St. Andrews Cathedral stands just outside the glassy mall from which I ascended. Soon I enter another less glassy, not-quite-so-contemporary shopping mall combined with a hotel of towers that compete with the density of towering buildings, scraping the sky as they say. Big city sounds, traffic, and scores of people off to somewhere or another. The guitar shops are in the basement and I find them after filing through corridors of knock-offs – jeans, shoes, cowboy boots, belts, and used camera shops. A tattoo parlor is busy. I turn a corner and the first shops appear, loaded with guitars (Figure 2). It becomes apparent that the basement holds a cluster of guitar stores, and before long familiar sounds, songs, and sights excite me. Even though I am so far from home, I can find all of my favorite guitars and amplifiers, famous and not-so-famous, conventional and "boutique" brands, in great abundance. It is a feast, and I plan to indulge.

After some time in Davis Guitar, I venture onward and discover a "vintage" shop with gems from guitar history (Figure 3). There are guitars of all ages, representing the milestones in music history associated with the amplified "electric" guitar. Acoustic guitars are available as well, but my interest is in the loud and amplified. To say I was surprised would have been an understatement. I had not counted on a treasure hunt, but there I was, looking at some really amazing artifacts in various conditions. Obviously the guitar had history in Singapore, history, and the history of guitar gear that I have accumulated over the years provided a ethnocentricity just waiting to be opened to other guitar histories. I spent some time in Guitar Connection looking and then asking to try out those guitars more easily accessed.

Actually communicating with store personnel led to equally familiar questions and exchanges I have had elsewhere. The language of guitars and

Figure 4. Davis Guitar, the oldest and largest guitar store in the basement of the Peninsula Shopping Centre. Photo by author, 2011.

Figure 5. Guitar Connection has an amazing collection of vintage instruments. Photo by author, 2011.

amplifiers is global, and gear talk sounds the same, with local history, desire, needs, and contingencies vibrating right along with the steel strings. While strolling Guitar Connection I met Wayne, a guitar tech working on an instrument in a small room at the rear of the store. Long-haired, young, skinny, wearing jeans and T-shirt; once again, a uniform that makes sense for the electric guitar corp. We strike up a conversation, and Wayne hooks me up with a few antiques that I play through equally antique amplifiers. I lose track of time and place for a few brief moments while reflecting on this unexpected encounter. I laugh at myself – Well, what did you expect? This is Singapore. I chuckle as I consider the sense of exotica that informed my own surprise to find guitar shops stocked with the same guitar good life that I too desire and know.

Thanking Wayne, and leaving Wayne's World, vowing to return ASAP, I head off, following the sound of "shredding" pulsating from inside another shop, actually a second shop space of Davis Guitar. Hunched over a purple-blue Greco Les Paul solid body guitar, screaming at low volume in complete overdrive is Burn, an employee of this small addition to the larger store. T-shirt and jeans, long-haired and skinny, this time bespectacled, adorned with chains and marked up with body tattoos, Burn shreds, that is, he plays heavy metal music, dense and thick with distortion, squealing, squeezed harmonics, dark and destructive sound meant to be in your face, ears, and body.

Figure 6. Guitar shops in the basement of the Peninsula Shopping Centre, Singapore. Photo by author, 2017.

I listen for some time and then strike up a conversation. I expected to hear this genre – I knew metal was popular in Asia from past experience, and from an emerging scholarship (Wallach 2008) on youth and popular culture in Southeast Asia. I ask Burn if he is in a band. He says he is, and I return with, "Where do you play?" "We don't," he replies. "I hate Singapore," he adds. As quick and sharp as his shredding, Burn tells me that Singapore doesn't allow "noise pollution." It turns out he is in a band for which there are few opportunities for gigs. Burn plays in a band that doesn't perform, at least in public venues.

Singaporeans often say that their island nation is densely inhabited by ghosts who are frequently disturbed by the never-ending construction that reshapes infrastructure and social life. On my first day in the basement of a shopping mall, among a collection of guitar shops and music stores, I encountered the ghosts of "yellow culture," disturbed not by the youth culture of the 1960s, but by the youth culture of the 21st century. On this very first day, I began a friendship and musical collaboration, I discovered a feature of local history, and was provided some insight on contemporary cultural politics in this urban nation. At the time I did not realize that I would turn my personal encounters in this sonic city into an anthropology of rock music and urban life. At the time I did not realize that I would become deeply engaged in "participant-experience" (Pink 2009) of sonic ethnography as both an anthropologist and member of a Singaporean band.

My first encounters with Kiang would lead to collaborations – musical and anthropological – that continue today. From these first encounters I traveled back in time to another Southeast Asian city in order to conceptualize my sonic ethnography of deep sound. From Java I returned to Singapore to complete my arrival at the shopping mall where I was introduced to the lives that I explore in the following chapters of this book. In the following I examine more closely the space of these first encounters – the basement of the shopping mall – as a crossroads that extends the common metaphor of Singapore as a "crossroads to the east." The crossroads is also important in the lore and history of blues music, the musical genre of the band, Kiang, James, and I formed in the weeks and months that followed our initial meeting. In the legends of blues music, spirits and devils await at the crossroads to buy the souls of those who desire to play the blues. In the worlds of Asia, human experience also can enter into assemblages of power, danger, knowledge, and fate. The basement of the aging Peninsula Shopping Centre is one such place.

The guitar shops found in the basement of the Peninsula Shopping Centre located in the old colonial center of town attract a diverse group of Singaporeans and others. Among these guitar shops, I came to know and become involved with a small community of musicians, fans, friends, and family who meet on occasion to jam, drink, have fun and engage a "cosmopolitan conviviality" (Mignolo 2000) characteristic of this city state and its history. A variety of languages, things that have traveled from all over the world, and people from many places and backgrounds cross paths in the basement of this shopping mall. The community of music lovers that is the focus of this book comes together among these heterogeneous movements. The vital energy of this cosmopolitan feast is its cosmopolitan nature. The spirit of the community of music lovers is harmonized to a great extent by Kiang. As bass player and founding member of The Straydogs, a 1960s English-language rhythm and blues band, Kiang in the dense presence of things – guitar gear from all over the world – embodies the connections of these things and people with both the past and present, and to some extent the future. His guitar shop that has since closed, and now the "Doghouse," a small shop and storeroom that he opened around the corner from the original shop operate as "spaces of engagement" (Cox 1998) where the cosmopolitan conviviality of this sonic community in this sonic city is assembled and made.

Figure 7. Lim Kiang and the author, Guitar 77. Photo by author, 2011.

The Peninsula Shopping Centre

Tucked between the elegantly whitewashed and refurbished colonial buildings of the Civic District, many of which house museums and art galleries, and the gleaming skyscrapers of the financial district of Singapore lies the relatively dated Peninsula Shopping Centre at Coleman Street. Intended as an upmarket shopping mall when it opened in 1980, housing an array of shops from sporting goods stores and travel agents to tattoo studios and guitar outlets, the place has evolved into an eclectic zone that is shared as an enclave by a diverse clientele, from youthful punks and aging rockers to ethnic Burmese migrant workers. In the basement of the mall, where the aroma from the food stalls is spread by the building's air-conditioning, several rows of shops display a range of wooden acoustic and shiny electric guitars behind their glass panels. My conversations with the owners and assistants of these shops led to familiar questions and exchanges about the cultural politics of music under decades of state paternalism.

This area of the basement of the Peninsula Shopping Centre is noisy, but not as noisy as one might expect given the quantity and density of guitar shops. Nevertheless, the jingle-jangle, and abrupt explosions of amplified guitar chords and riffs are commonplace. For the most part, various levels of pyrotechnical guitar wizardry featuring familiar styles of guitar play sonically spill out of the doorways of the various shops. Some of the shops are more user-friendly than others, allowing customers to try out guitar gear at various volumes for varying periods of time. The biggest and most successful guitar shop is the least likely to let customers play. The smaller, boutique shops specializing in a limited number of brands, and the shops featuring used gear are the most user-friendly, and so the noisiest.

The basement where the guitar shops are located spans the Peninsula Shopping Centre and the Excelsior Shopping Centre. The Peninsula Shopping Centre is built on the site of Coleman House (1865), which, along with the street it sits on, was named after George Drumgoole Coleman. Later Coleman House became the Hotel de la Paix offering Singaporeans first-class amenities including telephonic communication and fine dining. It is said that the hotel's taproom hosted Captain William Lingard and author Joseph Conrad's conversations in the 1880s. Another renovation before World War II in 1942 resulted in the Burlington Hotel, after which the property repeatedly changed ownership and purpose. After the war, shopkeepers moved in, and, in 1965, the building was demolished. In 1971, the Peninsula Hotel and Shopping Centre was built. Opposite the Peninsula Hotel is the Peninsula Plaza, built in 1981.

Like many of the "veteran shopping malls" in Singapore the Peninsula looks aged and perhaps "forgotten by time" compared to the many new, sparkling shopping mall palaces, some complete with ice skating rinks, cineplexes, and so forth that are deemed necessary for the contemporary shopping experience in this glistening Asian city. The Peninsula is a "strata-title" mall co-owned by different groups of people. A strata-title mall allows owners the freedom to lease their shops to any tenant who is lured by the relatively lower rents, which is why it is not unusual to find similar businesses in the same building.[22]

The Peninsula's location in the central business district is prime. Descriptions of the shopping mall promote the "slew of pleasant surprises for the shopper looking to garner quality bargains."[23] Mall promotions and advertisements note the mall's "colourful cosmopolitan history."[24] An internet-based travel site offers the following description of this cosmopolitan Southeast Asian crossroads:

> At first glance, Peninsula Plaza seems like an unremarkable mix of money changers, travel agencies, and souvenir shops. It's not until you're inside and can see the signs in the beautiful, curving script and get a whiff of the fish sauce that permeates the air it is clear that Peninsula Plaza has become a home-away-from-home for Singapore's Burmese community. The clothing shops sell traditional longyi (a sarong), convenience stores stock Myanmar Lager, and there's even a Burmese-language library.[25] Customers in online comments characterize the mall as a place "for all your Burmese (Myanmar) needs! All ethnic groups of Burna [sic] congregate here (Shan, Chin, Kayin, etc.) A food court at the basement, ticketing agents for your travels in almost every floor!" (Ted Patrick Boglosa, October 14, 2014.[26]).

In fact the shopping complex is known as "Little Burma" providing services, food, and shopping to a Myanmar community over 50,000 strong, making some space in this place as a "home away from home" for this community. While standing at the crossroads of current movements of people in the Southeast Asian region, which is the result of travel benefits for citizens of ASEAN countries including few visa restrictions and extremely competitive regional airfares among budget airlines, the mall also is described by some customers online as "a very hobby-centric mall – lots of music, photography & sportswear shops" (Benjamin Ng, July 24, 2011).[27]

Among the international brands stocked by the guitar shops in the mall, there are also makes and models specific to the region, for example from China and Australia. Finally, the Japanese versions of international brands of guitars are more abundant here than in North America, given the regional flavor of the guitars in the basement stores, and, of course, the proximity of Japan to Southeast Asia.

The density of guitar shops and the outstanding overall representation of new and used gear attracts Singaporeans, regional travelers, and foreigners working and living in Singapore, along with those travelers from further afield who are interested in browsing guitar shops while in town. Two shops especially demonstrate the diverse gear available: Guitar 77 and Guitar Connection. Guitar Connection deals in "vintage" instruments and boasts one of the most outstanding collections of rare and hard to find examples of classic globally known makes and models that I have ever come across. Open for 14 years, Guitar 77 also dealt in used and new gear, which increases interest from a crowd looking for something unique and different compared to the common gear found in the shops that only sell new instruments.

This combination of Southeast Asian regional and global connections of people and things make the basement a site and space of engagement where heterogeneous movements and the re-assembling of humans and things simultaneously haunt and make place. This basement oasis for the guitar-minded gear-lover provides shoppers and music lovers, and especially the community that congregated at Guitar 77 (and now the Doghouse), that "vitality and periodic capacity for surprise in a variety of nonhuman force-fields," which Connolly (2013: 400) describes as a foundational insight of the "new materialism" in the social sciences and humanities. Guitar stores, guitars, and guitar gear are "invested with differing speeds and degrees of agency" that energize the appeal of the objects themselves (ibid.). In fact, the lure, as any guitar lover will tell you, is the belief that all of these "objects" have the potential to live a "clearly multiple and complex life" in these "sites" and in others (Latour 2005: 80). In fact it is this very "fragility of things" that is vital to "differential periods of stability, being, and relative equilibrium" in the emergent social in this basement oasis (Connolly 2013: 400). First impressions, not surprisingly, in the basement of the Peninsula Shopping Centre are sonic – the place is heard before it is visually encountered no matter from which direction one enters.

Upon our first meeting when we recognized each other as blues men, Kiang and I jammed and exchanged a recognizable "cosmopolitanism" that was stunning in its degree of similarity. As youths we listened to much of the same music. Together we were able to determine this immediately – and sonically. After plugging in and playing for some time, Kiang and I had communicated. Our social was mediated sonically, a thing in and of itself dependent upon the connections and movements of my fingers in relation to the fretboard, the pick used for plucking the strings, the strings, the pickups, the guitar, the amplifier, the electricity and so on. Kiang and I began to know each other before speaking, or at least we emerged socially for each other in the midst of sonic exchanges mediated entirely by things and our actions with them in hand, in sound.

Steve and Kiang Guitar 77.mov

Figure 8. Sonic encounters. Simulation of first jam on "Stormy Monday." Still photo from film by Sun Jung, January 2012.

English Language at a Crossroads in Sonic History and Experience

Modern Singapore has always been and remains a multi-lingual society. At this crossroads, languages and dialects, and, obviously, sonics meet and mingle from all over the world. In the spirit of "racial harmony," the Singaporean government has, since its inception, recognized four official languages that represent the CMIE scheme used in the legibility of ethnicity in this multicultural, cosmopolitan city state. Mandarin, Malay, Tamil, and English are the official languages, with English taking precedence in a vertical mosaic of linguistic diversity. Kuo (1978) notes that English received its dominant position over the other official languages in the spirit of racial harmony, its centrality to the colonial project, and its status as an international language of modernity. The selection of and emphasis on English can be attributed in part to the functions it served in the newly emerging nation state. English as the language of educational instruction was in part a response in the heady days of independence to the fear of communism that dominated the affairs of the state (Hong and Huang 2008). In an attempt to quell mainland Chinese interference and regional communist factions, the government limited the use of Chinese in educational instruction, merging Nanyang University with the University of Singapore as a method of linguistic control for the cultural politics of the early state (ibid.). Singapore was a hub of trade and commerce formed during the period of British colonialism, and English had been and so remained central to the business and finance communities operating on an international scale. Lee Kuan Yew (1950) argued that the "returned student," the overseas-educated Singaporean, was obligated to be a part of an independent Malaya and the formation of its government. These "returned students" were central figures in many of the anti-colonial movements around the world and most had received their tertiary education in western, English-speaking institutions, where they encountered the English language's status as an international language of modernity.[28] English in the colony and in post-colonial Singapore operated not only as a language of the elite, but ironically became useful horizontally as a lingua franca in this diasporic community. These "functions" of English among the inhabitants in this crossroads established the prestige of English language use (Kachru 1983).

Another important function that English has served is as a language for artistic and literary expression (ibid.). Yasser Mattar (2009) focuses on "domestic English-language music" in Singapore as a linguistic basis for sonic "authenticity" in the reproduction of rock music, and other western popular music. For this community of musicians, English-language rock and roll and blues are the genres of choice when jamming and performing. In the 1960s, The Straydogs and many Singapore bands emulated and covered English-language pop and rock music. This sonic similitude, in addition to the sound and amplitude of rock music signaled and amplified not only the authenticity of the imitations performed by Singaporean bands when they covered these songs, but also resounded the cosmopolitan modernity that was and is Singapore. Today, Kiang, and the rest of us jam and perform English-language rock music whether as covers or in our original music we write and play.

The majority of this community, and especially the older members who were youth in the 1960s, grew up in English-speaking households, with Chinese dialects, Malay or Tamil as community languages. This heteroglossia, both linguistic and cultural, provided Singaporeans opportunities to shift codes depending on context, genre and expressive form: speaking and singing Chinese dialect in one, Malay in another, English in another and so forth. Some are better able to accomplish this code switching than others. Nevertheless, it exists as a general feature of Singapore's speech community. Singlish, a prominent form of English used among the members of this community, is a creole that is unique to Singapore, synchronizing a version of English within and among grammatical and lexical features of Mandarin, Chinese dialects, Malay, and so forth.

To this extent, English has been "nativised" (Bhatt 2001: 534), allowing Tan, Ooi, and Chiang (2006) to characterize Singapore as a "non-Anglo native

English speaking country." This native version, in the minds of many Singaporeans, and in the minds of those Singaporean musicians who jam and perform English-language rock music, is not authentic but also not necessarily inferior. For the sonics of rock music, the sound of Singaporean English as it affects rock music vocals can pose a problem. Those who become singers are often able to sound like the native English-language singers who provide the vocals for the songs that bands cover. Sounding like an authentic English speaker in these sonic works of imitation selects those in the community that can accomplish this sonic challenge. According to Mattar (2009) because of the manner in which English is spoken in Singapore, the English-language rock music made here never quite lives up to rock music made in countries where the genre originated – Europe, particularly the UK, and the United States. This "double consciousness," or "always looking at one's self through the eyes of others" (Du Bois 1903), and in this case through the style and sonics of singing English, is pervasive, and shapes musical practice in this community as well as the opportunity to perform in Singapore's music scene.

I became the singer of our group, Blues 77, and the current singer of The Straydogs because I sound authentic. This isn't the only reason, but the authenticity of my singing led me to be selected to perform this role in the two bands, even though I consider myself a poor singer. My singing voice oscillates in the low registers, growling out lyrics with raspy, smoky overtones. Coupled with the sounds I make on the electric guitar, the bluesy authenticity of my vocals authenticated my expression of the blues; and in Singapore as recognizable of the genre of beats and blues.[29] It should be remembered here that Kiang recognized me as a "true bluesman" when he heard me play guitar. Later I confirmed this when I sang "Stormy Monday," a blues classic that we still play today. At this crossroads to the East, and in the basement of the mall, also a crossroads, English operates simultaneously as a great harmonizer, a gate-watcher, keeper, teacher, monk in contemplation, and guardian of the boundaries through which authenticity and modernity are deployed among the community of musicians central to this book.

This double consciousness in the reproduction of English in song does not extend to speaking. Musicians return to Singlish when talking to the crowd, or making statements when jamming and performing. The code switching involved between singing and speaking requires differing values oriented around authenticity. Speaking Singlish, or simply using the local accent associated with Singaporean English, actually works to mark bands as local, authentically Singaporean bands made up of Singaporean musicians. These sonics of authenticity allow cover bands that play a western rock repertoire to selectively localize the music as Singaporean, or at least to localize cover songs played by an authentic Singaporean band. In this way musicians and audience, together, deploy double consciousness for their own purposes, and in the process create a local music.

Blues, Rock, and Cosmopolitanism at a Crossroads

English-language bands perform a repertoire of classic blues and rock music as well as contemporary popular music. For the generation of men and women that make up the majority of the community I observed, classic blues songs and rock classics from the 1960s, '70s, and '80s dominate set lists and jam sessions, especially those from England and the United States. The music scene in the early 1960s in which The Straydogs formed and performed was dominated at the time by a band from England – Cliff Richard & The Shadows. The Straydogs deviated from their counterparts who were making music under the influence of The Shadows, directing their attentions to other English and American bands that played music classified as "blues rock" – the alternative as an audience member at one of our later shows described in a conversation with other audience members (personal communication, Jamie Gillen November 7, 2015).

Local music historian, Joe Pereira, author of three books on the 1960s music scene in the region, describes a crossroads of sound and place during that decade. Joe and I had several conversations together on the topic, and he was a co-presenter with myself and Kiang on a panel held at ARI that explored "The Resilience of Vernacular Heritage in Asian Cities."[30] In his presentation, Pereira described the Singapore music scene in the 1960s and '70s for the audience of mostly academics and researchers. He also gave public lectures that coincided with our Straydogs performance at the Esplanade. The following description of the Singapore music scene during the "swinging sixties" is drawn from his talk at ARI.

Pereira's research reminds us of the significance of the 1961 Cliff Richard & The Shadows performances at Gay World Stadium over two nights in November 1961. Previously known in the 1950s and '60s as the Happy World, and renamed in 1966, Gay World Stadium hosted many "cultural shows." In addition to the usual movies, operas, cabaret, sports, and shopping, Gay World Stadium, billed as the greatest covered stadium in Southeast Asia, could accommodate as many as 7,000 spectators.

The stadium had a dance hall with a dance floor that could accommodate 300 couples. Gay World supported various forms of dancing for a cosmopolitan diverse ethnic audience that was and is Singapore. Singaporean Malays and

Babas alike danced Malay *ronggeng* and *joget*, and Gay World offered a special *ronggeng* kiosk (a bandstand) where Singaporean men could find dance partners. Gay World Stadium was far from being a world-class venue. It had no air-conditioning, and was more suitable for sporting events. Nevertheless, it had stadium-like seating and it hosted an event that heralded the beat movement in Singapore. Singapore in the 1960s did not have venues that could support rock music performances and performers from England and the United States. Promoters had to make do with venues that at least could seat large numbers of people. When the Rolling Stones played Singapore in February 1965 they appeared at Singapore Badminton Hall in Guillemard Road, another sports venue refitted for popular music performances.

With the rise of the pop music movement in Singapore in the early 1960s, various sonic crossroads appeared. The Cellar, a basement restaurant located in a bank building began to have Sunday tea dances that featured the Checkmates, fronted initially by Shirley Nair and later by the singing duo The Cyclones. The weekly tea dance sessions held on Sunday afternoons attracted immediate interest. The size of The Cellar was restrictive; once capacity had been reached the doors were closed (actually a wrought iron gate). Those not admitted caused trouble with the staff and management. The management decided to end the tea dance sessions at the end of 1964. Fights and brawls at the stadium events, in addition to similar problems associated with the popular music scene provided fodder for government concern and local police action, leading the public to associate popular music with local violence.

There were other venues that continued to host the tea dance sessions. The Golden Venus Club was another basement club owned by the Orchard Hotel located at 2 Orange Grove Road. Tea dance sessions at the Golden Venus began in early 1965. The host band was the Checkmates with a line up of singers that included other local musicians, in particular The Cyclones and Vernon Cornelius. Cornelius had been a vocalist with the Trailers who played tea dance sessions at Katong Palace. In later years The Straydogs would replace the Checkmates as the host band for the Golden Venus tea dances. In addition to the clubs and cellar restaurants was the plethora of British Military camps dotting the island. These camps had messes for officers and other ranks as well as youth clubs for children of serving soldiers. As the pop music craze took off with Merseybeat, these service clubs wanted bands to play at their clubs. Promoters scoured the island for bands to play at these venues and there was no shortage of takers because the gigs paid well. These venues were to become important places for Kiang and the others to develop and practice their craft. The military circuit also provided opportunities for Singapore pop musicians to travel the region, playing at the designated R & R locations 1960s. With the build up of the American War in Vietnam, Singapore was designated as a Rest & Recreation center. There were four venues that catered to the American soldiers. Ria Country Club in the east coast and Shelford Hotel in Shelford Road were reserved for officers while other ranks had Newton Towers and Serene House.

Singaporean musicians socializing with British and American soldiers resulted in a sentimental education of sorts. In these social contexts Singaporean musicians tuned into trends in music (fashion, etc) that were mostly unknown among most Singaporeans. Bands were requisitioned to play at these venues and in the process were introduced to not only 1960s English-language rock and roll, but also soul and jazz music, country music, and other genres circulating the region and globe at the time.

Soon the hotels saw that there was an opportunity to cash in on this trend and began to book pop bands to play month-long residencies in the hotels' clubs. In 1964 the Goodwood Park Hotel booked The Quests to perform there, and their appearances there were a sellout. The monthly residencies in the clubs became barometers for musical trends, featuring the latest in "hip" styles of music, fashion, but more importantly, as actualizations of cosmopolitan ways of life; actualizations in performance and in cultural consumption that were thoroughly Singaporean in spite of the so-called origins of these popular trends. By the end of the decade the venues for popular music began to dry up. The British clubs dwindled as the British announced their pull out from Singapore and the bases closed, beginning 1968 and ending in 1971. The US government took Singapore off its list of designated R & R centers and stopped rotating their troops to Singapore in 1970. Singaporean popular music bands lost significant places to perform. Also in January 1970, Singapore's government announced the blanket ban on tea dances. Popular music performances continued with month-long residences for Singaporean bands. However, the acceptable musical genres led local bands to cover mainly commercial music. As Pereira has pointed out, "this was the situation then at the end of the decade." (Joe Pereira, November 6, 2014, Singapore).

John Wu, writing on Vernon Cheong's excellent blog documenting his experiences in the 1960s music scene writes:

> We baby boomers in Singapore in the 1960s also wanted what the teenagers in America and Europe wanted, a better life than what our parents had when they were young. Looking back, the world in the 1960's [*sic*] was ripe and ready to be conquered by Western artistes like Cliff Richard and The Beatles. Their pop music symbolized the new life, the good life, and we all wanted a part of it. We were young, our future

was ahead of us, we didn't have to worry about paying the bills, that's [*sic*] for our parents to worry about.[31]

As Pereira and others illustrate, the global wave of rock and roll that was first associated with contemporary youth cultures was also taking root in Singapore by teenagers keen to appropriate the energies and lifestyles of their western counterparts. This is where the stirrings of a new post-war youth-inspired cosmopolitanism in Malaya was beginning through rock and roll. In an interview with Kiang on February12, 2012, he tells me the story of how he became attracted to music played on electric guitars and drum kits. His story is not only influenced by family, friendships, neighborhood life, but also by the language politics of the time as the Singapore Story began to unfold. He and those who became associated with The Straydogs lived in the east coast of Singapore in Katong, and while his mother spoke dialect (Hainanese) his household was an English-speaking one through and through. Kiang relates that this "English only" household shaped his listening experiences and the kinds of music he was exposed to as a youngster. He describes the east coast as a place where "educated" Singaporeans chose to reside at the time of independence. A higher level of education and speaking English were tightly entwined. The radio he and his friends listened to and the government schools they attended reinforced the dominance of English in their daily lives. He says, "We only listened to western music."

I ask, "How did you get started in all this?" Kiang relates a sonically mediated story of brothers, family, girlfriends, and social popularity. His sister was dating William (William Tan), the then soon-to-be original guitarist of The Straydogs. William brought a guitar along while visiting Kiang's sister. Kiang, in his early teens and younger than William, was dazzled by the sound, by the older peer, by the thought of a world of boyfriends and girlfriends. Kiang says, "I fell in love with the sound of it, and he was playing some Shadows." Kiang relates how William played some "licks" from a Shadows tune and Kiang immediately knew he wanted to learn the guitar. He was already keen on music prior to his emerging social awareness at 15 years old. His house had a piano and he could pick out tunes he heard on the radio. His family recognized his natural talent, while his sisters took piano lessons and struggled, he was able to play the piano by ear.

"So this guy that was dating my sister, my brother who was the vocalist, they met up with Ronnie the harmonica player, and Jeffrey could play a little guitar. They always hung out at the beach." These friends and siblings formed a band. His older brother was not so keen on Kiang's joining the band; he didn't want his younger brother following him around. However, when William showed up with the guitar, Kiang was ready to be swayed by all that it represented: emerging adulthood, social popularity, entry into the "new world society" sounded by a sonic history beginning to sweep the globe. His parents didn't object to his youthful musical leanings but times were tight, so if he wanted to pursue this fancy he had to do it on his own. Moreover, Kiang describes this group of teens that included brothers and friends as "filial kids." "Every night we went home, and we respected our parents. That is the way we were brought up," he says. In fact, his father, known among the friends as "The Chief" continued to play a guiding and at times disciplinary role as the band formed and began a performance career. Kiang describes the motivation in the early days of the band: "We just did it for fun, loving the music and just wanting to be different. Being a musician was really different in those days. Not everyone played like they do now."

An element of this difference was the ability to tap into the cosmopolitan currents of the time. The guitar and the band were signs of this desire and capacity to actualize and participate in sonic seductions and global lifestyles. Clothes were also crucial signifiers in a signification system for which capitalist consumption was the method for accumulating wealth, power, and prestige as well as a sense of the cosmopolitan.[32] Pereira, the Singaporean historian, is also an amateur musician and a contemporary of Kiang. He has interviewed and written about The Straydogs. I had coffee with him one afternoon and he remembered what drew him most to The Straydogs in those days: "They had the best clothes. Those clothes, those wonderful clothes." The semiotic circulations of fashion styles along with sonifications of post-colonial modernity in Singapore were the basis of forging not only new identifies for youth and other Singaporeans but new modes of participation in history. As Shiva Choy, a Singaporean blues player who was active as a youth at the time remarked in an interview for Pereira's book, *Legends of the Golden Venus*, "the more you sounded like someone else the greater hero you became" (1999: 18). Siva Choy's social imaginary of heroic sonification as he remembers "the 60s" as "a time we had to discover everything ourselves" (1999:17) was forged within the belief that a young Singaporean man could share in the same cosmopolitan attitude and optimism that characterized Singapore as a crossroads to a cultural and global modernity while remaining locally anchored in a thoroughly Singaporean cosmopolitan conviviality.

Pereira describes in his books (1999; 2011) and in our conversations over the years the cosmopolitanism that was at the root of the Singapore music scene when Kiang and his brothers and friends formed The Straydogs. Emerging from colonial history as the British Empire's crossroads of the East, Singapore as a crossroads continued, in this case as a crossroads where western popular music for many young Singaporeans at the time acted as a "great harmonizer" in local cultural modernity. Just as the father of blues music, Robert Johnson, received the ability to play the blues on his guitar after selling his soul to the devil at the crossroads, Kiang, The Straydogs, and other local bands sold their souls to learn how to play western modernity for themselves at this Southeast Asian crossroads. Some learned to play the English popular music of the time resounded in the music of Cliff Richard & The Shadows. Others, like The Straydogs, learned to play the "beats and blues" music emerging in the American music scene at the time. In both cases, these local Singaporean musicians and bands made this cosmopolitan music their own, domesticating it for both non-local and local audiences that reflected the kind of mimetic alterity that was and continues to be something more than mere imitation.

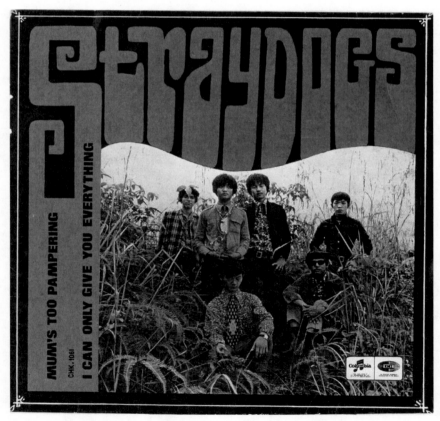

Figure 9. The Straydogs and their clothes, 1967. EMI single release.

The current scene is not much different from that of the 1960s. Covering music from American and European bands still dominates the performance and jamming scene. However, as the musicians from this golden age have aged, set lists for performances and jam sessions have evolved to include classic rock and blues from the 1970s through the 1990s. When contemporary English-language popular music is covered by younger musicians, the repertoire is equally more contemporary and not so classic, and the audiences are younger as well. But for these aging rockers and the community they are involved with, bands from the past remain central for establishing repertoire and communicability among musicians, especially for jam sessions. Everyone can play "Smoke on the Water" by Deep Purple (1972), Eric Clapton's version of "Little Wing" (1970), or "Hey Joe" performed by Jimi Hendrix (1966), to name just a few. This common repertoire provides for sonic and social cohesion effervescent in either mechanic moments of solidarity among members of the community or a touchstone in the organic solidarity of everyday life in an urban milieu.

Walter Mignolo (2000) considers cosmopolitanism as a counter movement to globalization. The Straydogs and a small but energetic host of Singaporean bands sounded Singapore's locally established engagements with global pop culture at the time of national awakening. The vibrant music scene Pereira documents is this island nation's objects in waiting that when activated remind that Singapore has always been at the center of cosmo-politics immersed in a kind of "planetary conviviality" – a conviviality for the cosmopolitan forged across vast global networks, and in this case a conviviality whose structure of feeling – a sonic resonance – was formed and remains firmly anchored in post-colonial Singapore today. The Straydogs and other 1960s Singapore bands represent locally produced sonic studies of global history – then and now – engaged in what anthropologist Steven Feld (2012) refers to as "acoustemology" – a "way of knowing the world through sound." The sonic cosmopolitanism I encountered forged from a historically situated conviviality continues to be expressed acoustemologically. But more importantly, the cosmopolitan conviviality I have experienced with Kiang, James, and the others over the course of these years and a variety of projects is enacted, fostered, and maintained through numerous large and small, formal or trivial reciprocal exchanges – reciprocal exchanges like those that emerge and were enacted in jams and performances – that require compromise and sacrifice. The communitas involved submerges social status and background in favor of egalitarianism. Leadership is emergent and task-oriented. In both cases, egalitarianism and leadership, there is potential for this egalitarian play frame so essential to the life-hood of this community of interest to dissolve. Those of us who are better off, economically, provide resources to others when needed – paying for drinks, food, airline tickets, and hotels. Taking the lead in music making can generate negative consequences, sonically and socially. At any rate, taking the lead, whether this involves proposing a tune to jam or perform, making decisions about solos, soloists, singers, arranging rehearsals and performances, all provide opportunity for the egalitarian ethic to become a comparator for measuring the actions of people. This moral economy is sonically experienced in jam sessions, rehearsals, practices, and performances during which sound and sonic capabilities exist in constant, ongoing reciprocal exchanges that emerge to guide musicians through the obligations involved in music making. Participating as a band member requires showing up, knowing the parts, stepping in and out when necessary to let others contribute, balancing skill levels and competitive urges in a sonic commensality that is also the basis of the social cosmopolitan conviviality that is the ethos of this assemblage of musicians, family, friends, and fans.

As I learned from the *kroncong* rehearsals in Indonesia, the sonority of a moral economy resounds in its "locality"; a locality in this case involved in past and present worlding exercises. The music making, in the past and present, represent "ontological choices" that can be "actualized or not, within themselves and outside of them" (Descola 2010: 336). And while compromise and sacrifice are unevenly distributed relative to emergent networks that have within themselves different affordances and requirements among things and people, it is this egalitarian conviviality, remembered as "embodied history" over and over again in a presentism of jams, rehearsals, and performances as well as the other associated forms of sociality that is valued most of all. It is this sonic cosmopolitanism – sonorous exchanges – that remains central to these lives. Its existence as ethos affords Singaporean musicians and audiences creative opportunities to ascribe fully to the "cosmopolitan commitment" (Mignolo 2000), framed at the same time in an intense loyalty to Singaporean identity. In spite of decades in which many of Singapore's 1960s music legends, until recently, appeared at best as a marginal aesthetic footnote in the Singaporean story.

Selective Localizations at a Crossroads

As Kosambi (1962) noted Mother-Goddesses (Mother-companions) were housed at the crossroads in the Vedic literature. These Mother-Goddesses had the ability to speak different languages, thus produced localized opportunities for domestic offerings to be made to family deities and ancestors of passersby from many different backgrounds. In this way the crossroads was transformed from a place of movement to a locality over and over again. Just as Robert Johnson received his ability to play his local black American music in the song "Crossroads" at a place where "Didn't nobody seem to know me, everybody pass me by," the community that hang out in the basement of the Peninsula Shopping Centre selectively localize the sonic circulations and articulating networks of things and people. Domestic offerings are made, and the domestication of heterogeneity takes place. "Selective localization" as Watson-Andaya (1997) illustrates, is a common feature in the history of Southeast Asian peoples. Local groups have throughout time adopted and re-invented the historical currents, winds and flows of other cultural traditions that have traversed this Old World, and later global crossroads.

As Kiang and I got to know each other, I spent more time at Guitar 77. Over time I became acquainted with its music scene and that of some of the other shops in the mall. I discovered that nearly every afternoon and especially on weekends, a group of regulars gets together in Guitar 77 to drink and jam. These happy hour jam sessions are loud gregarious affairs in which sonic presences are exchanged and food and alcohol are consumed. These domestic rituals in which sound, sustenance, and consciousness are central to the minute self-transitions from an everyday life of work, to one of being-in-the-world as a musician – a jammer – reproduce a cosmopolitan commitment fostered by song repertoire and gear as something uniquely Singaporean.

Happy hour in the shop, band rehearsals, and performances follow a structure of experience known in Singapore as "talking cock." Yoa (2007: 123) describes, "talking cock" as "garrulous affairs" in which "the visceral and the public" meet and "assume a fetishistic form" (Yoa 2007: 123). The "rocker" and the rock and roll lifestyle as it existed and configured in both the past and present are the focus for interaction and identity formation in response to the normative citizenship promoted by the Singaporean state. Talking cock is a visceral pleasure among men in Singapore. As Yao notes, talking cock in Singapore is "exuberant talk and masculine boasting, lubricated by delicious food and abundant alcohol" (ibid. 2003, p. 127). Intense, sometimes fiery, and often explosive language and ideas are conjured mostly in reference to the demands of the Singaporean state and the contingencies of daily life in Singapore. These happy hour jam sessions provide intense and condensed social times to live the convivial cosmopolitanism of The Straydog style that balances a cultural critique of the Singaporean state and the cultural politics it supports with the set of tropes condensed within the figure of the musician and in particular the male rock musician. The happy hour jam sessions, that take place in The Doghouse since Guitar 77 closed, are just one example of "domestic rituals" in which sonic offerings amidst food and drink are made to the cosmopolitan ancestors of rock music's history in Singapore. The happy hour jam sessions operate to localize the crossroads for all those who pass by.

Figure 10. The bar is open. Afternoon jam sessions at G77. Photo by author, 2011.

The social that emerges from the afternoon happy hour jam sessions connects with cosmopolitan sonic history that, as Gramsci might say, serves this "community of interests" in their own "way of thinking and feeling." Another mode of selective localization actualized as domestic ritual in this basement place is the yearly celebration of Chinese New Year at the shop, and now at The Doghouse. In the public hallway outside the shop's doors Kiang organizes the yu sheng, known as "lohei yusheng" or simply lo hei (Cantonese) in Singapore. This salad made of fish served with daikon (white radish), carrots, red pepper (capsicum), turnips, pickled ginger, sun-dried oranges, lime leaves, Chinese parsley, chili, jellyfish, chopped peanuts, toasted sesame seeds, Chinese shrimp crackers (or fried dried shrimp), five spice powder and other ingredients, laced with plum sauce, rice vinegar, kumquat paste and sesame oil, for a total of 27 ingredients, celebrates past, present, and future prosperity, mostly in terms of wealth. The salad toss is performed by those who have come together, each using a pair of chopsticks and making loud announcements of the coming of prosperity (Huat ah!), each person tosses the salad into the air above the dish at the same time. All who have joined in the lo hei eat a plate or portion of the salad.

Figure 11. The lo hei for Chinese New Year in the basement of the mall. Photo by author, 2012.

Lo hei is a strictly regional cultural practice found only in Singapore and Malaysia. Many Singaporeans in homes, offices, and so forth participate in lo hei. For those who assemble at Guitar 77, lo hei is a way to remember themselves as Singaporeans. The salad toss is part of the action for the social to occur, and the social in this case is open, attractive to, and interested in the potential and coincidences that occur at crossroads. The salad toss not only marks local experiences but is a local experience forging the crossways of life into places where local potencies of prosperity might be encountered. The salad toss in the public hallway of a mall turns this space into a place where a selectively localized social is made and remade over and over again in the public sphere. The salad toss stands as a "meritorious public work" that takes place in the presence of the vulgar displays of capitalist reality the basement of this shopping mall and the density of retail shops are organized around. The social described here is hardly distinguishable from the moral economy actualized in this representation, this experience in and of the ethos of this community. Amidst the consequences of capitalism – a basement of a shopping mall inhabited mostly by retail – the lo hei is a device of saturation in which participants experience the ethos of the community based on an economic ethic of mutuality and reciprocity – the very foundation of the cosmopolitanism conviviality at play. The "movement, motion, mobility" that Teo observes (2018: 21) as central to the Singapore Story that suffices as everyday "common sense" in this "shining Global City," a common sense that Teo notes (ibid. p. 20) "gets under the skin." The mutuality and reciprocity that are conjured as the social of jam sessions, performances, holiday celebrations, and so forth appears in this logic as stuck in time, or at least out of tune with capitalist movements that have come to define life in this "amazing" city state. Once again, at this crossroads opposing yet complementary forces – human and non-human – assemble over and over again as networks anchored in differing histories and experiences that pass through. The guitars, the customers, the stores, the cash – the retail lives of these things – rely on the continual renewal of experience without history, so essential to the reproduction of capitalist consumption. The happy hour jam sessions and the lo hei transform this logic of capitalism by localizing all of these things, and so in the process afford localizing opportunities for all participants.[33] History, community, and heritage become severely inflated as the social of the jams, happy hours, and activities like the lo hei take place. The lo hei, like the crossroads, in the basement of this mall signal the confluences of human movement in associations, in assemblages where encounters with great harmonizers, gate-watchers, keepers, teachers, monks in contemplation, guardians of the boundaries, devils, and other harmful entities are likely. The lo hei occurs in the hallway for pragmatic reasons, but also because the hallways themselves flow in ways that crossroads often do with the social potential involved. For these specific lo hei, The Straydogs heritage and Singapore's cultural history become inseparable, only recognizable together as one.

For Pickering and Green (1987: 8) such communities are organized, and such activities as the lo hei occur in a "vernacular milieu" that can be "can either be dispersed or relatively confined to particular localities" as "situated sources of identity." For Kiang and I in particular, and for the others in the community, the recognizable cosmopolitanism referred to as the "60s" that provided an initial medium through which we could communicate, opened up to a historically anchored, locally rich Southeast Asian sonic cosmopolitanism that Kiang and others played a part in resounding during jam sessions and happy hours. From basements and guitars shops, to bars and band tours and concert stages. A kind of vernacular heritage consciousness, not unlike the "customary consciousness" E. P. Thompson (1993) explores in England in the 18th and 19th centuries, becomes for this small community of music lovers and makers an effervescence of "customary consciousness" in which a way of knowing the world through sound, an "acoustemology," "becomes a right protected." A right to another Singapore story, one left unsung in official discourse, but that resonates and resounds in the streets of this city state. The chapters that follow, then, write a sonic ethnography that explores the deep sound of urban lives.

Chapter Two

Katong

"Katong"
I walked the streets of Katong
Heading for Jago Close
Along the way I don't skip some place
Like David's record shop
Along that muddy street
Cut through Ronnie's backyard
Into Kuo Chuan, on to the beach
Stop by Jeff to lure him out
The kopi kept on flowing
The ciggies they were burning
Into the night, harp's a wailing
And we'll be screaming twist and shout
Chorus:
Yeah from Kow's Red House on rainy days
We'll gather at the Cold Storage Cafe
Having steak, eyeing Lily all day
And it seems to me like we're having fun
Watching all the girls go by
Some are pretty and some are not
But it's alright
The years just crept on by
You go your way, I go mine
Parts unfixed at every turn
I'll soon be 65
Through the years we kept on dreaming
To finish what's left undone
This empty feeling kept on playing

Inside all our minds
Soon this feeling will be over
When we pick up those guitars
Stubby fingers, creaking away
As the breathless harp wails
Chorus:
Yeah from the Red House in Katong on rainy days
We'll gather at the Cold Storage Cafe
Having steak, eyeing Lily all day
And from the rooftop of Stangee
To Ah Pui's at the beach
Not going to make the news
Straydogs being busy
Born to the blues
Oh yeah,oh yeah, yeeeeeeaaaaahhhhhhhh
(Lim Kiang 2005)

Coming of Age around Jago Close

The Straydogs were a Katong band. All of the brothers and friends that formed
the band walked the streets of Katong: a "close-knit community that transcended
racial and ethnic lines" (Phua and Kong 1995: 133) located along Singapore's
east coast. Considered the "traditional home of the island's Peranakan (Straits
born Chinese) community" (Shaw and Ismail 2006: 189), Katong's colonial
history begins as a plantation area, and later as a recreation retreat for rich
Chinese towkays (businessmen) (Phua and Kong 1995: 117). Katong in the
early 20th century transformed into a "wealthy suburb" where English-language
education was established with the area's first school (Telok Ayer English
School) in 1923 (Phua and Kong 1995: 118). With the demise of the
plantations, the east attracted Eurasian families, a migration that was encouraged
in part by the English-language schools and the establishment of the Holy
Family Church in 1932 (ibid. p. 118). While Peranakan patois was in common
use in Katong, Peranakans were also fluent in English (ibid. p. 130). This
cultural history of urban development in Katong led to a family life in which
the use of English was common (Shaw and Ismail 2006: 189), and a community
that was cosmopolitan in outlook and demeanor. It was within this cultural
geography of Singapore's east coast that Kiang, his brothers, and friends formed
The Straydogs in 1966.

Kiang's song lyrics identify features of Katong's built environment and its coastline location that at the time was within a stone's throw of his neighborhood. Since 1965 land reclamation has pushed the coastline far from where Kiang's family and friends lived. Kiang's song, "Katong," resounds a life near the beach. In the 1950s and '60s Katong's built environment developed as an "active retail and entertainment hub" (Phua and Kong 1995: 121). Kiang's lyrics capture some of this urban activity. Ah Pui's coffee shop located near the beach, the Red House Bakery located on East Coast Road, David's Record Shop, and the Cold Storage Cafe were the heart of Katong's built environment and the soul of those days of coming of age. The variety of cuisines concentrated in Katong reflected its 1960s cosmopolitan flavor.

Phua and Kong (1995: 131) found in their study of local culture in Katong that interviewees noted the cultural effect the Eurasian community had on Katong's structure of feeling as an open community that participated in a "friendly, neighborly, relaxed lifestyle." They also found, in addition to these characteristics of the community, an emphasis on the "strength of social bonds" established among residents as well as recognition of racial harmony that defined the community (ibid.). Kiang's and James' stories of Katong reflect this Katong culture. Now, 50 years since forming the band, their social ties with childhood friends remain strong. For our 50th anniversary performance (2016) at Hood, these social ties were put into action as old school friends came together to help organize the show. Lunches were held in order to plan for the show that mostly devolved into remembrances of the days spent as youth in Katong. The lore of place took priority over determining performance set lists, ticket prices, and show finances.

Kiang's family and friends reflect Katong's development into a residential suburb, populated by an English-educated middle class. It should not be surprising that Kiang and others in the neighborhood were attracted to 1960s English-language popular music. The original members of the band comprised of Katong's cosmopolitan Eurasian and Straits-born Chinese ethnic roots. The seaside location and mixed ethnic business community provided the atmosphere of openness that I have found as a significant personality trait among The Straydogs and among their friends from those days.

A Drive around Katong

One afternoon Kiang, James, Jan Newberry, and I went for drive around the old neighborhood. As we approached Katong from East Coast Road, Kiang and James began pointing out places haunted by ghosts they feared as youth, lawns they used to cut with sickles, the locations of past timber and logging operations along the river, remembering Eurasian dishes such as devil's curry, and so on. We turn onto what they describe as the "rich man's road" and marvel at the old homes along the way. James remarks that the area is known for its "good feng shui."

We continue to drive. Kiang announces: "That's the start of Katong." I notice a club I've heard about – Jazzistic. Kiang responds that he played there recently with his Pink Floyd tribute band. The police, responding to complaints, arrived to shut down the band, but stayed to listen to the music. His rocker rebellion continues where it began.

We pass a row of landed residences. Kiang remarks they are "priceless." We pass Katong Shopping Centre; "One of the oldest," James points out. "The first shopping centre," Kiang adds. "Katong has always been a rich area ah," Kiang explains. James points to some bungalow houses and tells of a house that was haunted and empty for many years. James, as long as I've known him, is a magical realist, finding the fantastic in everything, everywhere.

Kiang takes us to the Red House in the heart of Katong, "Where we hung out," James adds. Kiang begins to sing the lyric from his song, "From Kow's Red House on rainy days...." Suddenly James interrupts, "That was the record shop." In fact many musicians at the time hung out in this bakery.[34] We pass a road that led to Kiang's primary school, Seraya Primary School, a "pioneer primary school" that merged with Fowlie School in 1986, and merged again with other schools to form Tanjong Katong Primary School, a popular school with expats. James laments that Seraya has been torn down.

We pass the police station, the old Cold Storage Cafe, and a shop site of an "old Malay cobbler." We are traveling along East Coast Road where the hang out places mentioned in Kiang's song were located. The Cafe and coffee shop are now gone. We are on our way towards the Holy Family Church and Grand Hotel that are near Kiang's old neighborhood. As we pass the church, Kiang points to a business area that used to be a field where he, Jeffrey Low, and others played football. The location of a photography shop is pointed out by both, and Kiang says that the owner lives in America, and that they remain in contact to this day. The photo shop owner took photos of the band for their record covers. One of the photo shoots took place in a graveyard. James remembers the photographer's mom was not too happy because "she was superstitious." Excitement begins to build as we near our destination. Kiang informs me that I must take photos once we arrive.

We drive along a wide asphalt avenue that was once the beach. The Grand Hotel, no longer a hotel, faces what was once the coastline. It seems impossible.

Reclamation and urbanization of the area has completely transformed the built environment. Jan Newberry comments that Kiang and James, now in their late 60s, have witnessed remarkable change in the built world of Singapore during their lives. James responds, "When we were young we were bitten all the time by mosquitos. No dengue, no malaria. In fact, we caught mosquito larvae to feed our fish you know." Talk turns to reclamation. "From here all the way to Changi Airport is reclaimed land. It really changed our map," James explains. James remembers the sea being shallow in this area, where you could collect shrimps and prawns.

We arrive at Jago Close, a street where Kiang grew up that runs parallel between Kuo Chuan Avenue and Chapel Road where Kiang lived. The residences are single story bungalows, very distinctive to Singapore and I'm surprised that they still exist in this skyscraper, HDB apartment city. With small yards and fences, each house is built in the same style. A kampung feel for sure. Kiang talks of a Katong where doors were always open, and he and his friends could cut through each other's backyards to meet up. I can imagine a neighborly atmosphere with the coastline just off where the road ends.

Figure 12. The residences at Jago Close. Photo by the author, 2016.

At the end of the road there is a small park that sat on the coastline next to the Grand Hotel, still facing in the direction of the sea but at a great distance. Kiang shows us his house, and the house of his friend Jeffrey Low, also an original member of The Straydogs. Standing all alone in the middle of the park is a large tree. "Oh my god, the tree is still here," Kiang says with great surprise. Under this tree boys became of age. Ah Pui's coffee shop was located nearby, a favorite hangout.

Figure 13. Reclamation: the tree near Ah Pui's coffee shop at the beach. Photo by the author, 2016.

Sitting around this tree Kiang and his friends learned how to inhale Lucky Strike cigarettes, drink alcohol, talk about girls, recount brawls and fights with others in the neighborhood. I take a photo of the tree and send it to Kiang via email, after which he sends it on to others. Kiang emails me later that day describing how the photo has sparked memories. "Lim clan love the pictures. The Tree is now hot topic. Thanks." As Kiang's brother-in-law remarked in an email I received: "This tree has quietly observed many memorable moments in many of our lives. If only it could speak! Then again, maybe not!"

Figure 14. Kiang and "the tree" in Katong at the end of Kuo Chuan Avenue. Photo by author, 2016.

"This is where The Straydogs hung out, smoked," Kiang laughs as we park the car and approach the park at the end of the road where the beach once began and the tree still stands. "If you wanted to have a fight you came here," James adds. "Our stone table was underneath this tree, and this playground used to be the coffee shop, Ah Pui," said Kiang as we walk towards the tree. "You can see the Grand Hotel there," James points out. Jan Newberry asks pointing at the single story houses on Jago Close, "How did this not get developed?" Kiang responds, "Private property, not owned by the fucking government." He laughs. A sign posted on the fence in the parks says "For lease." Kiang calls the number posted on the sign thinking the park was for lease. He's told no, it was one of the houses that during The Straydogs' days rented for $30 a month, now renting for $3,000 a month. We all laugh.

Kiang tells a story of a built environment for which the tree was a central feature:

> Talking about Ronnie, ah, you know Katong, our houses we never keep the doors closed. During those times we would just walk and cut through his backyard. Life was so different then, people trust each other so much. Walking into people's houses. A Malay come into my house, no such thing as all this halal thing and all that. So during those times Ronnie's house was on Kuo Chuan Avenue, I'm coming through the block, cut through his house, go to the next block, Ronnie would nicely follow me, and then we reach Jeffery's house at the end of the road, call him out, go to Ah Pui at the beach. The tree, yeah, at Ah Pui, this nice coffee shop that sells ice kacang. Hang there, smoke a lot, drink a lot, smoking all sorts of nonsense. (Lim Kiang October 15, 2016.)

As we get into the car to leave Katong we pass St. Patrick's School – "my school" Kiang remarks as we pass by. James adds that during the Japanese occupation many people were killed in front of the school. Many of Kiang's friends were his classmates at St. Patrick's. When I play with The Straydogs, memories of this school always emerge. The bonds formed in the neighborhood, at school, and of course in the band remain strong today. This vernacular heritage formed through proximity and experience provides the cohesive force that keeps these aging men together even though all have moved away from Katong and on to other occupations. But when together, Katong always appears as a specter of times made and shared together.

Many of the places we visited on our drive around Katong are also identified in Phua and Kong's (1995) interviews as landmarks, as touchstones of meaning and identity for those who live in Katong as well as those who don't. The schools, shops, hotels, shopping mall, restaurants, bakeries, and coffee shops, churches, and bungalows by the beach comprise the topophilia in the interviews and during our drive. Kiang and James add haunted houses, trees, yards, stone picnic tables, and rooftops to the list. Food was mentioned often in the Phua and Kong's study as well as during our drive. Peranakan, Malay, and Eurasian cuisines dominated food talk along with the baked goods and curry puffs from the Red House bakery. And of course there was the coffee at Ah Pui's and Jago Close coffee shops. The variety of flavors indexes the variety of ethnic groups living together in the "culture area" (Phua and Kong 1995: 122) that is Katong. The cosmopolitan conviviality I discovered in the basement of the Peninsula Shopping Centre was embodied early on in the lives of this generation of Singaporeans who came from these streets of Katong. I found among these Singaporean "pioneers" the same neighborly, easy-going openness that interviewees in Phua and Kong's study cite as characteristic of Katong. This attitude towards being-in-the-world played a significant role in the formation of The Straydogs as an English-language rock band in the 1960s, and continues to play a significant role in manner and atmosphere of the community of musicians and friends that gather around Kiang. In this way the vernacular heritage of Katong remains present as a cohesive force around which a community builds itself.

Performing Katong

Katong was evoked during rehearsals for The Straydogs' reunion performance held in 2015 at the Esplanade in Singapore, and in 2016 at Hood to celebrate the 50th anniversary of the band. Katong also appeared during the performances themselves in expected and unexpected ways. Palmer and Jankowiak (1996: 227) argue that performances are "the collective and intersubjective construction of imagery through expression and experience." As "visible evidence of cultural production" (Mahon 2000) musical performances are meant to be seen and heard. This visibility "evokes and solidifies a network of social and cognitive relationships existing in a triangular relationship between performer, spectator, and the world at large" (Beeman 1993: 386). The Straydogs' performances, both in the 1960s and in the 21st century are "cultural performances" (Singer 1972) that are experienced as "spectacle," that is as Beeman suggests "performers," in this case The Straydogs, "present themselves as representative of a larger group or a larger reality" (Beeman 1993: 379). I propose that The Straydogs' performances both in the past and present make a spectacle of the cosmopolitan conviviality Kiang, James, and the others embraced as modernity in this Southeast Asian city when they were teenagers, and they do so by performing 1960s Katong. Ronnie, a Eurasian Singaporean harmonica and keyboard player now living in Australia; Jimmy, a South Asian and Chinese Singaporean guitarist; Kiang, a Chinese Singaporean bass player; and James, a Peranakan Singaporean drummer, embody the cosmopolitanism of Katong. In fact when The Straydogs perform, the assembled members cannot avoid this presentation of a world at large.

As decolonization proceeded and the nation state emerged, one of the central concerns of the newly formed Singaporean government was racial harmony. This concern was a colonial one as well, and continues today as a defining characteristic of Singapore. The government and Singaporeans alike need to avoid civil unrest and violence among and between the myriad ethnic groups that live and work in Singapore. Since the founding of the nation state, an important social engineering technique implemented by the government has been to classify and categorize ethnic diversity in Singapore using a rubric that distinguishes between four sometimes five broad ethnic categories. The acronyms CMIO, and CMIEO designate Singaporean citizens as members of Chinese, Malay, Indian, and Other, and in the case of CMIEO, the Eurasian category is present. This rationalizing of "Singapore multiculturalism" is used to account for Singapore's ethnic diversity as census data, but also operates in government schemes to engineer racial harmony by making sure urban areas and high rise residences meet quotas, linked to the percentages collected by the census, that establish both "racial" diversity and harmony throughout the city (Ye 2016). Many argue, including Kiang and the others, that these schemes have actually produced a hardening of the differences between ethnic groups leading to fewer interchanges between ethnic groups than there were in the past. Scholars and Singaporeans mark the 1979 Iranian Revolution as having a severe influence on ethnic relations, represented in the increased presence of Muslim clothing and headscarf use among Malays, and Malay Singaporean demands for halal food that made it difficult for Singaporeans of different ethnic backgrounds to eat with Malays.[35] As we drove around Katong this gastronomic politics made its way into our conversations.

When The Straydogs perform, they literally and figuratively represent a world at large in Singapore when ethnic mixing, especially in Katong, was considered by many I met as more relaxed than it is today after 50 years of socially and politically organizing Singaporean citizens into broadly designated ethnic groups. At the 2015 and 2016 performances the ethnic diversity embodied by The Straydogs was especially apparent in the audiences as well. From personal observations, I have found this is not always the case for many of the other musical performances that occur nightly around town. Malay bands play mostly for Malays, Chinese Singaporeans attend English- and Chinese-language live music venues, Indians are rarely found at either. The "European" community of "others" also has its own live music venues that it frequents. The 2016 50th anniversary show at Hood produced a highly diverse audience that is unusual in the music scene. Many approached me after the show commenting on the make-up of the audience.

When the band performs they perform a cosmopolitan conviviality that is especially characteristic of Katong, and in this way Katong is always present in spite of the fact that none of the band members live there anymore, or visit the neighborhood with any frequency. But The Straydogs performance at the Esplanade Concert Hall (November 4, 2015) conjured forth Katong as an urban community in another way. We were booked as one of three bands from the 1960s for the Esplanade's "A Date with Friends" series. Bands from the 1960s were featured as Singaporean sonic heritage during 2015, the 50th birthday of the nation state. The three bands were chosen as representative bands of the days of the tea dances held on Sundays in Singapore mostly for British and American military personnel during the 1960s. The three bands were also selected because each was well known to have played a legendary club known as the Golden Venus. Singer Veronica Young, the "Connie Francis of Singapore," opened the show. The Straydogs followed, and Vernon Cornelius, known as the "Cliff Richard of Singapore" and lead singer of The Quests, closed out the concert. Veronica, Vernon, and The Straydogs all held sway at the club at different times during its history. The club was located in the Old Orchard Road Hotel, an area in Singapore where many expats lived and worked. Rachel Chan describes the tea dance phenomena in an article written for the *Straits Times*:

> Contrary to the name, no tea was served at tea dances. Rather, tea dances were the forerunner of what is known today as 'clubbing.' If you were a teenager or young adult back in the day, chances are you would spend your Sunday afternoons at dance halls and clubs checking out members of the opposite sex and dancing to live music played by popular local bands such as The Silver Strings, Keith Locke & The Quests and Bobby Lambert & The Dukes.

The Straydogs were also among the bands that regularly played at the tea dances. Chan continues, "Popular venues included Golden Venus (formerly located at Orchard Hotel), Prince's Hotel Garni (now Park Hotel Orchard) and South East Asia Hotel (formerly in Waterloo Street). Non-alcoholic drinks were served at these dances and the cover charge was $3, a princely sum in those days."[36]

For some reason Vernon, during his performance, decided that the audience wanted to hear stories rather than music, and devoted much of his allotted stage time to a stream-of-consciousness rant. It was during this rant that Katong appeared. As the MC and the producer of the show fumed backstage about Vernon's monologue going over the time allotted for his performance, Vernon decided to slight The Straydogs publically. As his band performed the same chorus and verse over and over again, waiting for Vernon to start singing, he stated:

> It was my greatest pleasure to perform at the Golden Venus because it was Orchard Road. Yeah… and when a group from Katong came to speak with Lawrence [bass player for a mainstay Golden Venus band known as The Checkmates] to say can we play at the Golden Venus, Lawrence says to this group – Hello, this is Orchard Road. This is not Katong! Orchard Road was a little more high class than Katong back in '65. (November 6, 2015, Esplanade Concert Hall, Singapore.)

We were watching all of this unfold backstage on a TV monitor with Veronica and her band. We can only speculate why he decided to denigrate The Straydogs before the audience, but both bands agreed that The Straydogs had just "killed it" onstage before Vernon went on, and this energetic performance and audience response had annoyed and unsettled Vernon as he waited to perform. Whatever the reason, Katong appeared in Vernon's monologue as a class-based rendition of Singapore's urban space. As Fanon (1968: 36–37) famously described, "The colonial world is a world divided into compartments... a world cut in two... a Manichean world – light and dark." Junjia Ye (2016: 93) notes that, "Until the 1960s, Singapore's population mostly lived in separate ethnic settlements established by the colonial administration." Limin Hee (2005: 53) describes Orchard Road prior to the 1960s as "an area of airy colonial bungalows." This compartmentalization of Singapore's city space was an extremely visible experience in colonial and post-colonial Singapore in which enclaves, like Orchard Road, represented class and race differences. Orchard Road continues to resonate as a site of foreign embassies and upscale shopping. The Esplanade concert as spectacle presented the audience an "existing order's uninterrupted discourse about itself" (Debord 1994) performed as a nostalgia for the 1960s. As Debord argues (1994), a "spectacle is not a collection of images, but a social relation among people, mediated by images."[37] While spectacles may present a worldview in iconic fashion, they are nevertheless performed as "the collective and intersubjective construction of imagery through expression and experience" (Palmer and Jankowiak 1996: 227).

Unlike The Straydogs', Veronica's and Vernon's set-lists were made up completely of cover tunes. And when either sang they did their best to imitate the vocal attributes of the original singers. The Straydogs performed a mix of covers and original material with me providing most of the vocals in my raspy American English. However, Jimmy Appadurai-Chua performed and sang a blues classic "Stormy Monday" and Lim Seow, Kiang's older brother and founder of the group sang a 1960s Them's classic "I Can Only Give You Everything,"and a Straydog's original, "Mum's Too Pampering" that came out as an A and B side of the Straydog's first single for EMI Records. A colleague of mine attending the concert reported that when the Straydogs began to play, an older gentleman seated next to him turned to my colleague and said that The Straydogs were "alternative music back then." Veronica's and Vernon's performances were complete with costumes and costume changes by each, and the music was performed at moderate levels of amplification with a Las Vegas quality to the styles of performance. The older audience loved hearing the hits from the old days and sang along. The Straydogs, on the other hand, performed at higher levels of amplification and, if not Straydogs fans, audience members likely did not know the original material performed by the group. We were sandwiched between these somewhat glitzy, kind of cheesy Old Orchard Road imitators, producing a spectacle that actually captured a slice of Singapore music scene history revealing class distinctions in taste and performance style. Vernon, in his comments, provided verbal art to the singing and music that instantiated these social differences marked out in urban space.

Vernon's performance ended suddenly when the MC saw an opportunity during one of his costume changes to dash onto the stage and announce that Vernon was returning to the stage to perform his "last song" of the evening. Vernon upon hearing his time was up became livid and stomped off the stage to scream and swear at the producer. The police were called and arrived as we were leaving, with the producer heard to say that Vernon will never perform at The Esplanade again.

Katong for Kiang and the others proved to be a cohesive force in the solidarity these friends maintain today. Katong life and their experiences provided the focus for many of our conversations, for the stories and memories shared during our drinking sessions after rehearsals, and at the planning meetings for the shows. Every time, in these contexts, Katong came alive again as a vivid spectacle visible in stories, words, and memories of exploits that not only bonded these men together even after 50 years of differing life opportunities and paths, but also as a kind of vernacular heritage around which the group organized themselves on occasions. For Kiang, James, and the others, Katong was a kind of seaside paradise. For Vernon it was a class-specific urban space that did not live up to the high culture of Orchard Road in 1965. Katong for the members of The Straydogs was the urban place where cosmopolitan modernity arrived and was experienced. As teenagers living in this area of Singapore, The Straydogs encountered the signs and sonics of a global urban modernity. The worldly cosmopolitanism was localized as tea dances, in music recordings of Singaporean bands heard on the radio, by televised programs that debuted in the early 1960s such as Talentime, in amusement parks, radio programs, concerts, and performance venues where this sonics of global modernity could be heard. These cultural features of the 1960s in Singapore were filtered through coming of age in Katong, and it is this amalgam of cultural influences and circuits that continues to resonate for this small music community today.

Chapter Three

Sonic Scales and Urban Life

Spatio-Sonic Scales in an Urban Milieu

Sonic existence in Singapore can be challenging. Chinese opera performances were moved to the outskirts of town. Tamil ritual drumming was outlawed. The Islamic call to worship has been confined to the congregational inside the walls of the mosque. Musicians and bands of all styles and kinds until recently have found extreme limits on opportunities to perform music in public. Throughout the life of this Southeast Asian nation state, public sonics have been a source of concern and a target of social disciplining since independence and statehood in 1965. Bart Barendregt (2014), most recently and brilliantly for the region, and Lily Kong (1999) specifically with regard to the Singapore, explore the popular music scene noting the significance of the sonic politics in the various similitudes of modernity present during nation-building.

State concerns over "noise pollution" are manifested politically and spatially in the form of permits and zoning codes allocated to spaces and city places. State authorities designated spaces and various architectures of the built environment as educational, recreational, retail and so forth. Sonic parameters and tolerances translated into spatial dimensions and proximities depending upon the prevailing allocations of designations at any one time constitute an ontology for "spaces of dependence" (Cox 1998), organized as state sponsored urban planning in a "politics of scale" (Harvey 1985) in which sound is a crucial determining feature. Recently Kelvin Low, Jim Sykes and others have explored "the spatial politics of noise" (Low 2014) in this city state. Their work highlights the role of the state in urban affairs of life through legislative and licensing procedures that manage social conflicts produced by different kinds of sonic activities through the organization of socio-spatial presences as well as absences. Low (2014) examined 20th-century newspaper accounts and letters to the editor that complained about noise disruptions of daily life, and noisy performances Singaporeans found annoying and in need of regulation. Malay weddings held in the void decks of towering HDB flats are a commonly cited annoyance. Sykes (2015) also notes a sonic cultural geography in which certain ethnic groups and their spatial locations of residence around the city are considered by Singaporeans and the state as particularly noisy. Tamil drumming associated with holiday celebrations is just one of Sykes' examples. With this and other examples, Sykes brings together sound and social relations as he maps a sonic geography for colonial Singapore and for the present.

This chapter explores how the local live music scene in Singapore assembles within state "reach" spatio-sonic scales, the amplitude and durations of which are responses to access to public space for live music performances on one hand and the difficulties of establishing, maintaining, and sustaining a live music venue in a challenging business environment on the other. These "spaces of engagement" are crucial sites with the possibility for engagement dependent upon "the politics of securing a space of dependence" (Cox 1998: 2) made available for sonic uses by the permit and zoning practices of the Singaporean state.[38] These spaces of engagement include the home, guitar stores, rehearsal spaces, and local pubs and clubs, in addition to state supported venues, for example concert halls, the National Youth Council, and other indoor and outdoor performance venues located mostly in downtown tourist areas.

The growth of this sonic geography in Singapore is driven by the increasing access for nearly all Singaporeans to musical gear of all kinds, for all purposes, that in the past was highly limited by consumer price, skill and knowledge, local availability, and the number and density of active communities of interest (musicians and listeners). This democratization of access to the many things used to make contemporary music of every genre, local and global, at home and on the stage, is central to the making and assembling of alternative urban spaces in this sonically challenged urban state. The effect of this sonic democracy is a multitude of spatio-sonic scales scattered around the urban state, the extent and duration of each to a more or lesser degree subject to chronic threats.

A Sonic Geography of Singapore

My ongoing participatory ethnographic research in which I have followed a small community of musicians, their families, friends, and various other kinds of social relations has led me to various spaces where Singaporeans can engage in "musicking" (Small 1998). Small, in accord with Feld (2012) and his acoustemology, describes musicking as a "way to know the world"; particularly "the experiential world of relationships in all its complexity." Musicking not only refers to "the relationships of our world... but as we wish them to be." In the various spatio-sonic scales in which musicking is engaged, social relationships are made and reaffirmed, sometimes splintered, and hopes and dreams imagined. From home to concert hall, the relationship between space and sound are organized as a "hierarchy of scales" (Harvey 1985) subject to the "reach" of the state. From the home to the concert hall, respecting the sound limits of neighbors and neighborhood and the Public Entertainments Act (PEA) that provides the process and guidelines for obtaining required licensing for live music performances in public urban spaces, provide for the dependence that regulates musicking in Singapore respectively is mandatory. From home to concert hall, the organization of spatio-sonic scales also extends the reach of sonically charged affective possibilities. Spatio-sonic scales active in various "spaces of engagement" emerge in what Harvey might imagine as "the struggle for the right to the city." In particular, this struggle for the city occurs in alternative urban spaces compared to the state sponsored concert halls and youth centers where state governed censorship prevails. The home, the practice spaces, pubs, and so forth call to our attention musicians and their communities who attempt to capture the commons of urban life "at a variety of scales" (Harvey 1985: 78).[39]

Home Musicking and Practice Spaces

Making music at home in high-rise HDB flat Singapore is a challenge indeed. Bothering neighbors with sound can lead to conflicts, tension, complaints, but also cooperation, tolerance, and reserve. One can hear children practicing piano, flute, and other school music instruments in the early evening hours. Electric guitars and drums are much less tolerated. However, bands are heard making music during celebrations, weddings, and so forth in the public spaces provided by the void decks on the ground floor of high-rise flats. Letters to the editors of Singapore's major newspapers regarding homemade sound are usually complaints that are often directed at the cultural practices of the three major ethnic groups that generate intolerable sound. Finding a place to play – to jam – is motivated by these spatio-sonic limits surrounding home musicking.

In spite of the limits that constrain music makers at home, technological innovations that allow for making music silently offer the opportunity for music makers, and especially those using amplification, to make music at home. Amplifiers complete with headphone inputs allow electronic musicking to be made silently, at least as far as the neighbors are concerned. One can play electric guitar, bass, and so forth with as much distortion as desired, at high volume levels and achieve the jam experience in one's bedroom. Feedback, gut-wrenching bottom end, screeching high-end distortion, crying wah-wah pedals can be experienced and heard in one's headphones. The jam and onstage experience, therefore, is reproduced silently. The sonic limits of making rock music in one's flat is mitigated and provides rock music makers the opportunity to practice, and so reproduce in part the sonic experiences associated with jamming and performing. And while this sonic experience is satisfying to a degree, and necessary to develop one's "chops" as a musician and jammer, it is the collective experience of jamming and performing where the most desirable sonic flow is achieved.

These residential spatio-sonic scales in which limits are mediated and mitigated by technological innovations, along with the desire to achieve collective sonic flow, generate the production of urban spaces in Singapore that allow for such sonic flow to exist. Scattered around the city are various jam studios and practice spaces available for rent by the hour where musicians can turn it up and jam collectively, or in some cases on one's own. Kiang and I booked time in such places for rehearsals and practice, both for The Straydogs and for our own band, Blues 77.

Figure 15. Jam space (Just About Music Studio and Music School). Photo by author, 2017.

Bodily Scales, Gender Performances, and Embedded Scales

July 7, 2013 (field notes)

A couple days of lead-up and rehearsal before last night's gig at Hood provides some insights. The day after I arrived, Kiang had arranged a rehearsal space for James, Kiang, and myself to practice. I made my way to the shop hours before the rehearsal to hang out, play guitars and talk. The shop holds daily happy hour at 6 pm, and the many people I have met among the group of local amateur musicians attend. These are "talking cock" sessions of men, young and old, who hang out and play music together in several different but connected bands that often share members. For example there is the Pink Floyd tribute band, there is Khan Kontrol, and our Blues 77. The members of these bands are members of other bands in town, mostly amateur, sometimes putting out CDs, but mostly looking for non-paying gigs just for the chance to play. Gigs among this group are intense times of alcohol consumption that go on until late. Almost always a group of men, but sometimes girlfriends and wives join. And while gigs and performances celebrated one form of Singaporean masculinity, the talking-cock intoxicated rocker, limiting, at times, women as full participants in the fun, nevertheless, women consumed alcohol and performed rock and roll music as well.

The bands then are local subgroupings, assemblages of sorts where man-hood, gender, race, ethnicity, nationalism and local lives assemble with some friction as these guys live their lives together day by day. Care for each other is given materially and emotionally in this milieu – but in the manly idiom. Kiang is everybody's uncle and he enjoys the role of elder who happens to have some legend associated with him because of the formation of his band in the 1960s – The Straydogs. While his over-the-top alcohol consumption is important to these manly times together, and of course to showing off his legend as a rebel rock star and blues player in a town that has continually tried to ignore and even regulate the "lifestyles" that are perceived to be associated with these music genres, the alcohol consumption can undermine his position as elder, as "uncle," as his demeanor changes and the likelihood of being offensive increases. But the offenses are somewhat expected, and it is the response that matters most. As an uncle he needs to accept everything and provide support, guidance, and unconditional love, so to speak.

At the end of the show we proved our manliness and our acumen as blues musicians by announcing to ourselves for ourselves, "We don't need no pedals!"

Sound, as Nancy (2007: 7) argues, is "made of referrals." "Meaning and sound" come to share "the space of the self, a subject" (ibid., p. 8). Sound is "the ricochet, the repercussion, the reverberation: the echo in a given body" (ibid.,

p. 40). As Pickering and Green (1987: 8) describe, The Straydogs and their associates present a "community of interest" organized around rebellious behavior and cosmopolitan conviviality. As amateur musicians involved in the music scene, Kiang and the others reproduce community in the "vernacular milieu" in which the "rocker" and the rock and roll lifestyle as it existed and was configured in both the past and present, provide a "specific plane" that becomes a focus for interaction and identity formation (ibid.). Such communities of interest can be numerous and exist on their own or come together collectively. This happens with blues jams that occur from time to time around Singapore. Local communities like Guitar 77 become involved in such events and encounter other communities that share similar interests. While Guitar 77 represents a "situated source of identity" (ibid.) it is also a recognizable one among the other situated sources of identity in the community.

Figure 16. Feeling it at a blues jam. Hood. Photo by author, 2011.

The vernacular milieu is the context in which participation in processes of cultural life and bodily performances of self and person thrive. In order to understand the situated sources of identity involved and the manner in which sources of identity are used, it is crucial to identity the technical phenomenon involved that help produce individual and collective representations of identity. The urban places that offer enactments of and engagements with these individual and collective forms provide the equipment for life to do so. In these urban spaces – the jam studio and the bar and pub in particular – jams and performances present limits and possibilities to specific constructions of identity formations associated with differing genres of music that Kiang and others use to evaluate and perhaps judge. For the making of rock and blues music by Kiang's generation, the rocker lifestyle is central. In addition to the gear, the stage and the sound, is one crucial source, a central source, alcohol. The consumption of alcohol, often whiskey and other spirits, is apparent as an important characteristic of being a man and the performance of masculinity. While the images, activities, and associations that surround the everyday life of this community of amateur musicians are cosmopolitan and include people from many different backgrounds, the nature of most activities undertaken can be characterize by the centrality of masculinity and male bonding. In the case of Kiang, James, and the community of interest in which they participate, a particular form of masculinity that is situated in structural time, performed within a social temporality – the jam sessions, performances, happy hours, and so forth – binds this group of men who were boys in the 1960s. The afternoon jam sessions in the store, the gigs in Singapore and on the road follow a similar pattern referred to as "talking cock." The performativity of this particular form of Chinese Singaporean masculinity involves this capacity to talk cock.

This gender performativity is expressed and experienced as bodily scales assembled within what I consider rather "conservative" configurations of gender relations within which heteronormativity and heterosexuality are clearly present. This preferred reading of gender and sexuality in Singapore, often attributed to Chinese, Confucian, patriarchal, Asian values, is a central organizing principle for state policy. The government's Housing & Development Board (HDB) programs are schemes by which the state provides subsidized public housing in a country of high rents, price per square foot, and land scarcity. Age (21 years old) and a heterosexual marriage that forms a "family nucleus" are basic requirements for access. The policy excludes unmarried Singaporeans (single, widowed, or divorced without children) until the age of 35. As Tang and Quah (2018: 648) illustrate, "Housing policy in Singapore is therefore configured fundamentally around the very narrow heteronormative model of a family, namely, the heterosexual, married, procreative couple."[40]

My own experiences and observations of "gender" and sex in Singapore, and specifically in the events and experiences described here were at times in my estimation old-fashioned, puzzling, and sometimes offensive. Of course there exists a great deal of variation. Kiang, James, and other "uncles" held what I would identify as old-school perspectives on gender and sexuality characterized as mostly chauvinistic, leading to husbands and wives living essentially in different social spheres. Church for example was something the wives nurtured. The jams, performances, rehearsals were men's affairs. And there exists, for both men and women, a distinction between those who are insiders and those who are outsiders. The wives, female friends and fans shared in the sociality as equals in this egalitarian community. However, masculine performativity overwhelms in all instances, and generally women, even though present, were inconsequential to many of the events and activities. What I mean is that the masculine performativity described here locally stamped and sonically reproduced in jams, performances, rehearsals, happy hour sociality, Guitar 77 and The Doghouse social events was for all of us – men and women included – significant degrees of intensity experienced by all in the effervescence of flow in any one of these assemblages and activities. Admittedly, most of my observations took place in social situations under the influence of often fairly high levels of alcohol intoxication. In these situations, some of the grossest and more offensive interpersonal relations between Singaporean men and women – from my perspective – took place. Chinese Singaporean women were publicly marked as available for men in a variety of ways. I was surprised at times by the direct dialogue occurring inside and outside music venues that objectified often intoxicated women by intoxicated men as essentially and only available for sex.

All of this said, women family, friends, and fans participated in all of the events, and nearly all of the activities described in this book. Veron, Kiang's partner was a most frequent participant. James' partner, a very infrequent one. Younger members of the community included partners with more frequency and as co-equals. Some of this gendered participation was shaped by class, as the egalitarian, cosmopolitan ethos celebrated by men was not enough to induce attendance by some women. Alcohol consumption and intoxication also contributed to the gender composition of events and activities, and their appeal beyond the participants of the core group of this community, did not seem to appeal to women in the same ways achieving altered states appeal to the men in this community. Similar to other research and my own experiences in the region, I observed while patriarchy is deeply rooted as the predominant point of view among Chinese Singaporeans on appropriate gender relations, on the ground patriarchy is often checked and balanced by matriarchy that emphasizes matrifocality in patriarchal households and social relations. I attended Kiang's family gatherings for Chinese New Year as well as other gatherings related to turns of life – marriage, birth, death – and was always struck by the Confucian take on basically Malay ideas about gender and relative social status.

Kiang often announced to the crowd as we finished our first song of the set that everyone was here "talking cock." Talking cock is a visceral pleasure among men in Singapore, especially Chinese Singaporean men. As Yao (2007: 123) describes, talking cock is "exuberant talk and masculine boasting, lubricated by delicious food and abundant alcohol." Intense, sometimes fiery, often explosive language and ideas are conjured mostly in reference to the demands of the Singaporean state.

> In the depth of alcoholic stupor, as dishes come and go, recollections of the salacious delight of the Bangkok massage parlour riotously meet reflections on the grand promises of the State and the wealth and power of the Lee family. The wild merging of subjects, the free marrying of the serious with the quotidian: these are the delights that have brought the men together. (Ibid.)

These are the very "delights" at the center of many of the activities that Kiang, I, and our associates find so pleasurable, and meaningful.

More importantly these "delights" nurtured at the end of the work day in the guitar shop jam sessions were sensed again – reproduced – in dense and intensified ways in the spatial scale of the club as live music. Storytelling that takes place adds to the noise and its politics. The following is a re-telling of one of a noisy story – a "vicarious image" (Attali 2009: 5) – involved in the play, performance, and so creation of this community.

Albi: Smoking State Secrets

Enshrouded by the plumes of smoke hanging out with musical friends I imagine typical Singaporeans – stereotypical ones I've encountered impressions of in conversations with professors characterizing the manner of student achievement in their classrooms, expat businessmen complaining of the lack of entrepreneurial spirit, Singaporeans themselves complaining of the absence of creativity. These national character studies agree on several personality traits exhibited by Singaporeans: Singaporeans are kiasi or "scared to die"; Singaporeans are kiasu, or afraid of losing out; Singaporeans emphasize family, hierarchy, and face; and finally, Singaporeans are stingy and rule-bound.

Much of what I have experienced participating in activities and associations that take place in the guitar shop when it was open, and now in The Doghouse, during rehearsals and band performances in and outside Singapore, does not line up well with these stereotypes of Singaporeans. Expat and local images paint the Singaporean as a rather dull, dour character with little creative potential. Foreign talent, therefore, is required for innovation. Risk evasion is seen as a sign of this submissive, passive personality that obstructs true, authentic creativity. Many Singaporeans I have come to know cite numerous excuses for these stereotypical personality traits. It's the fault they say of the state, embodied in educational institutions and approaches to pedagogy, work-related incentives, real estate prices, authoritarian management of daily life and behaviour, and so on. In this way the state effect is present in Singaporean and other imaginations of Singaporean selves and persons.

As the smoke cleared some, a couple of my friends shared a story while we continued to drink our whiskey. A couple of guys laughed that they were writing a screenplay, or perhaps the script for a play to be acted out upon a national stage. And, unsurprisingly, as I have come to learn from many talking cock sessions, the Lee family is front and center as targets of sarcasm and complaint. And as a circulating text the facts of the story are emergent, purposively manipulated in each story time is enacted with available storytellers and participants. The story of Albi is based upon Lee family members, but scrambles some of the "facts" of Lee family history and relationships. This version of the story of Albi reflects this plasticity.

Told as a three-act play, the story of Albi centers on a Singaporean who was the albino son of former Prime Minister Lee Kuan Yew. The first act finds the albino son named Albi interned upon birth in the basement of the Istana, the residence of the Prime Minister. Albi grew up in the basement never seeing the light of day, never leaving the basement. During his imprisonment Albi endured daily beatings from his father the Prime Minister. The Prime Minister also had another son who succeeded his father to the political office of Prime Minister. The old man, considered the father of the Singapore nation, continues with the daily beatings until his death. The other son, now Prime Minister, then continues the daily beatings, however, with increased and brutal intensity until Albi can take no more. Fed up with the brutality, Albi murders his brother. This event ends the first act.

The second act finds Albi released from his basement prison, finally wandering outside the Istana on a brilliant Singapore day. The second act revolves around Albi's encounters with everyday Singapore. Encounter after encounter, however, only reveal to him that even though Singapore is a "nice place," efficient and easy to find one's way around, he also finds that everyone is unhappy. The emergent quality of the story here appears as a theory of Singapore's state effect, something referred to by numerous tellers of this story as "equal unhappiness." This political science had been outlined for me while the band was performing on the road in Ho Chi Minh City, Vietnam. One evening before our performance the band members were sitting around talking Singaporean politics. My friend stated that political culture in Singapore is one where everyone has to endure defeat and so has repressed expectations – or as he termed it equal unhappiness. Albi discovers this state effect as he wanders Singapore marveling at its modern efficiencies but becoming increasingly distressed by an overwhelming depression among its citizens. This revelation ends Act Two.

Act Three moves us toward revolution led by Albi. In most renditions of the story, this act is the least elaborated and worked out. Mostly depicting naughty pornographic acts and events, revolution appears adolescent. Smoke begins to fill the air again as we laugh and devolve into jokes about penises, fellatio, and other depictions of uncontrolled bodily substances.

Whether risk averse or not, the drama here narrates the space of dependence the engagements reference, and so draw meaning from. The story challenges the state effect in creative ways, as works of the imagination that provide some level of cultural critique in the context of social practice. Making trouble and meaning in a basement corner of an aging shopping mall, in a local bar, in a jam studio between rehearsal breaks, in the dressing rooms of performance halls in Singapore, affords a small community of musicians, family and friends who gather to meet, drink, smoke, jam loud amplified music, eat, and perform as a band to transform the spaces of dependence into "spaces of hope" (Harvey 2000) where making sense of self and others exact possibility and creative potential within the limits of the official use of public space. Such experiences in storytelling, assembled in urban space with alcohol, friends, food, guitar gear, sound, music making, are the "local politics" Cox (1998) argues emerges in the concordances of spaces of dependence and engagement. Bodily scales are realized in cosmopolitan spaces in which local and global interrogations in dialogue, in space, and among things make for trouble and meaning. The conventional wisdom that Singaporeans are uncritical conformist, risk averse, and compliant participants in functional ensembles orchestrated by government or commercial enterprises is suspended in time and place.

These talking cock sessions on different scales with differing degrees of sonic and experiential intensity are assembled over and over again as personal yet cultural festivals of masculine cosmopolitanism of a certain generation of men who are Singaporean. As we followed musician friends from gig to gig, in town and in several locations in the region, in some way or another we made sense of our location in these ways. These "focused gatherings" featuring "messy fluid" bodily scales, position participants in the capturing of ontological scales around particular renditions of Singaporean masculinity that are anchored in some generational and ethnic depth.[41] For this small group, national scales of dependence were contemporary and historical, rooted in the urban present and past, fiercely criticized and chastised while at the same time being fiercely loved and honored. Jam studios, practice spaces, guitar shops, and bars and pubs as scaled technical arrangements provide a vital place for the "realization of essential interests" (Cox 1998: 2). These urban places as varying degrees of spatio-sonic scale assemble networks of "human and non-human" in durable yet innovatively respondent associations and resemblances in the reproduction of local meaning. The emergent quality of these urban places as performative space offer "an 'anthropological,' poetic and mythic experience of space" (de Certeau 1984: 92–93). Alternative urban space – popular milieu where urban residents engage in practice for themselves by themselves – is the struggle for the city in all of the senses.

Figure 17. Blues 77 live in the final days of the "old Hood." Photo by Ana Ferzacca, 2012.

Scale-ability: Hood From Keong Saik Road to Bugis+

> Old hood got a nice feel, people mix around with each other freely, kind of like home pub sort of place and the music is so close to the audience makes it very vibrant. (Kiang Lim, musician, February 2015)

Hood opened in 2011 and recently changed location (2013). Hood, a local live music club opened its doors for business on Keong Saik Road in the Chinatown district of Singapore not long after I arrived to take up an appointment at a research institute for my sabbatical. Until the 1960s, the area was a prominent and notorious red light district in Singapore with a high concentration of brothels located in the three-story shophouses known as examples of the "transitional, late and art deco styles" (Savage and Yeoh 2004). By the 1990s the area was transformed by the presence of "boutique hotels," shophouse renovations for private residences, coffee shops, restaurants, art galleries and other shops for commercial use. Hood's first home was a ground floor "shop" of a shophouse. Hood features local artists, not quite exclusively, but there is a preference for and concerted effort made to book local artists, making popular music ranging across most genres.

Figure 18. Entrance to the "old Hood" on Keong Saik Road. Photo by author, 2012.

Hood opened across the street from a well-known restaurant specializing in Singaporean Chinese food; next door was a popular Malay restaurant. Hood's emplacement among these historic restaurants in this particular neighborhood illustrates another feature of scale – duration. The topophilic hauntings of this place are saturated in generational depth especially for Chinese Singaporeans.

Along with the food establishments, a one-way street with sidewalks, make Keong Saik Road an appealing location for a live music club. Located just far enough away from high-rise residences that surround this heritage neighborhood in Singapore, Hood renovated its long and narrow premises to include a stage, a Plexiglas enclosure surrounding the drums as a buffer, a small bar, a few tables, an open area to stand, some outside tables off the sidewalk with ash cans for smokers, toaster ovens and microwaves to prepare a minimal menu. With so many of Singapore's well-known restaurants, food courts, and hawkers stalls so nearby there is no need for an extensive food menu (Hood allows outside food to be brought in). The most important item on the menu at live performances I attend with this group of musicians and their friends is alcohol – mainly scotch whiskey consumed by the bottle. However a wide range of alcohol is consumed; some generational preferences seem to pattern alcohol choices, although as the evening's performances proceed, a general trend among the crowd for shots and cheers emerges.

On the evenings I was present, the clientele was nearly entirely male. Women were present – girlfriends, wives, co-workers and friends of those who were usually playing on stage at some point in the evening usually made up the very small number of women on the evenings I observed. Women appearing to be out for a night on the town did filter through and were noticeable additions as they entered into a small, sometimes loud and highly charged participation by all, while other times Hood was completely empty. Generally, however, performers brought along family and friends, so an audience, even a small one, made performances at Hood feel like events. Hood provides opportunities for a wide range of talent, popular music genres, and age and gender of performers, except that local talent in town (as the sign says) is the determining factor in the selection of performers. Genres range from classic rock, contemporary pop, metal, and some blues performed at various levels of amplification from acoustic to electric instrumentations or some mix of both, by solo performers and bands. One evening I attended an event for high school aged music students. With each band a new set of parents and friends came and went.

Each performance generates a degree of the excitement of live music before an audience, performed and amplified at levels loud enough to call for nearly complete attention from all present. The only escape from this dense and intense sonic experience is out the front at the sidewalk tables, however, there you have to put up with the smokers. The size and layout of Hood, the sonic scale held grudgingly in place by the walls, percussing out the front door as it opens and closes during especially loud performances saturate the space with sound. Clement describes this sonic experience as "very vibrant."

The main difference is obviously the size of the place. We chose this place due to the location. It is central, and the shopping mall would be pretty crowded (at the time we signed the lease the mall was not ready). The place is bigger and it is more mass market oriented. To fill the place (or try to), we had to cater our music selection / decor / Food and Beverages to a larger audience. We couldn't be as niche as we were before. The decor remained the same, just bigger. The Food offering changed quite a bit as we have our own kitchen that is capable of dinner and lunch services. So we redesigned our menu from scratch. Our drink selection also increased because we expected a bigger crowd.[42]

Figure 19. Keong Saik Road (Chinatown), Singapore. Photo by author, 2012.

Bugis+ is a ten-story shopping mall located in the Bugis business district. The mall opened as Iluna in 2009, and after failed attempts attracting tenants and customers in 2012 CapitaMall acquired Iluna and renamed it Bugis+ With a unique metal mesh facade complete with lighting and streaming media, the architecture of the mall compared to the shophouse on Keong Saik Road couldn't be more different. Hood became situated in this new milieu that as a soundscape resounded of escalators, mall restaurants, and shoppers. And while Clement notes the "obvious" impact on the kind and quality of business jumping scales can produce, it seemed to me that there was more to this change in scale-ability. The move from Keong Saik Road to the Bugis+ mall was not only a change in classic features of geographic scale – size, distance, proximity, level – nor simply a scale of investment, risk, loss, profit, but a change in relations and perception. A "hierarchy of scales" purely economic and municipal became more visible. Clement the principal involved in Hood and Guitar 77, himself a well-known, excellent musician, notes this increased presence as he spoke of the "old place" as "less risky," "more cozy" but "impossible" in terms of scale-ability.

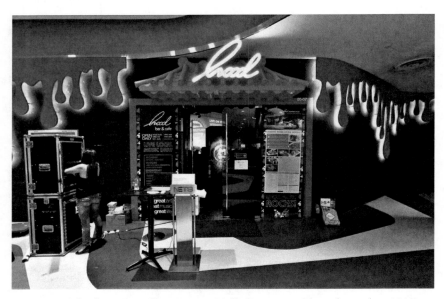

Figure 20. The "new Hood" in Bugis+ Mall, Singapore. Photo by author 2017.

The old place at Keong Saik definitely was cozier. It provided a more intimate experience for the customer. The revenue was limited by the size and the number of people [the premises] could hold. At the new place, the potential to earn more money is more, but we now are dealing with how to make this a cozy drinking environment. We can now hold events that cater for between 50 to 400 people. It would be impossible previously. The new place, being more mass market is also more scale-able. Now we are looking to do more events on top of our usual night business.[43]

Scale-ability, similarly disposed as spaces of engagement are formed within and from spaces of dependence in urban milieu, highlights the capture of, or at least the capacity to capture the urban commons, in this case contemporary Singaporean experiences and identities at, as Harvey notes, "a variety of scales." While spaces of dependence – the state, capitalist and commercial business relations – determine size and associated physical aspects of both locations as spatio-sonic scales, the spatial features on their own are minor determinants in their ontological capacities and network reach.

Clement and the newly located Hood jump scales sonically in a continued project that calls attention to localized social relations – local Singaporean talent. The "old Hood" offered a wide range of contemporary popular music in Singapore. Local talent was selected and the club presented itself as a live music venue for local Singaporean musicians. Associations with the guitar shop provided significant actualization possibilities for networks around guitar shop musicians and clientele to attend and perform at Hood events, jam nights, CD parties, and so forth.

In the new Hood, performance scale is expanded – stage, sound system, visual effects. Spatial location and physical distance of the audience is clearly apparent and demarcated: the stage is raised just above the audience's head level, rows of tables fill the space, there is a large section of the main room where patrons can be seated away from the music, and there is a smoking section outside on a balcony that overlooks the city street below.

The most obvious difference is that the new Hood is located inside a mall, with mall parking, mall escalators and mall shops sparkling here and there on various floors in large vertically soaring spaces. Hood is on the fifth floor, surrounded by several restaurants serving franchise food. A popular steak restaurant is Hood's neighbor. Unlike the local cuisine offered on Keong Saik Road, the food near Hood at the Bugis+ location appeals to a different generation. Hood's own menu also reflects its proximity to franchise food. It has been much expanded and now includes entrees. Parking is certainly more predictable and less of a hassle at the mall location; mass transit is nearby.

Figure 21. Clientele at the "new Hood." Facebook post. Accessed May 25, 2017.

From the perspective of some the Bugis+ location is more "central." Located between Queen Street and Victoria Street, the mall is surrounded by a number of churches, business and arts schools, the Singapore Management University is nearby, the National Library and several important museums. Bugis+ is also on the border of the Bugis arts and cultural district – the Bras Basah Bugis Precinct. This area was originally planned by Singapore's European founder to be the European enclave (and so the number of churches). The community quickly reflected Singapore's cosmopolitan foundations. The buildings of Singapore's former elite educational institutions are now home to museums, shops, and eateries, and repurposed to make sense in this emerging urban entrepot and its cosmopolitan history. Food and fashion, but also an entire array of thousands of Arabian nights for all the senses can be found.

Compared to Keong Saik Road, the depth of national, regional, and global scales are more clearly palatable, tactile, and visceral in and around Bugis+. Clement measured Keong Saik Road as "niche" – limited, in terms of scale-ability. Keong Saik Road, a one-way niche forged in structural time in the events of communities, Chinese New Year's for example, that reproduce generational depth anchored in a self-conscious community of interest – Chinatown. While this socio-spatial scale feels cozy to the mostly Chinese

Singaporeans who form the core participants, the scale-ability was also limited by the parochial qualities of the Keong Saik Road location. At least these are my impressions. The politics of socio-spatial scale that retrofits alternative urban spaces so that same qualities central to local communities extend and contain experience.

As far as I can tell, the national and regional scales forged in history within which Hood is now emplaced do not seem to have relevance to the owner, the performers and clientele I've come to know. Clearly apparent in the new location is a particularly local actualization of contemporary Singaporean sonic experience in which the interactive quality of live music is based upon current and therefore fleeting popular music. In this way global and regional sonic scales are tapped. Jam nights are a mix of local talent and hosts who can perform live nearly any current popular tune with the aid of iPads and other tablet devices that can quickly upload lyrics and basic chord structures from online resources while performing.

An enriched sonic democracy calls for some readjustment among bodies, nation, cosmopolitanisms, and live music experience. Kiang remarks that the "new Hood lacks the warmth and there is no mingling amongst the people."[44] Clement agrees, "Most of the guys prefer the old place... It was more of a hole-in-a-wall kind of place while the Bugis+ one is much more commercial."

Kiang and others who share in the networks assembled by the nexus of guitar shop–old Hood–new Hood engage – they show up, eat and drink, perform. This presence is not so much diminished, although this seems to be the effect at least on the occasions I've been present, but rather spatio-sonically scaled down. In both space and in acoustemology, the way of knowing, that was the old Hood, in the new location has lost some vibrancy. On the occasions I've been present, the group of friends and musicians I've learned from and played music with usually seat themselves as a group at a set of tables off to the left side of the stage, close to the bar. The remainder, and of course majority, of the tables extend across the front of the stage towards the back of the room, and then off into an area furthest from the stage. On the occasions I've been present and from conversations about the new Hood in many contexts, the general consensus is that a younger, dating crowd has come to populate Hood in increasingly large numbers. This is good for business. The sonic effect on the live music is audible: contemporary popular music, taking audience requests, audience participation in performances, the use of hosts to mediate audience experience, visual experience as alternative to sonic experience with the entire back wall of the stage being used as a screen to project live soccer matches while live music is performed. As Clement says, the "new Hood" is "commercial."

Figure 22. Musical performances at the new Hood. Photo by author, 2017.

Nevertheless, this group of friends continues to show up, eat and drink, and perform from time to time, some members of the group more than others. Opportunities to perform still exist and are extended when slots in the performance schedule become available. Local talent is still preferred. Hood continues to strongly endorse its networks and segments of the music community providing performance opportunities as well as becoming involved in production and management of some local groups, musicians, and singer-songwriters. The guitar shop and Hood are linked into networks of practice spaces, music schools, church programs, musical communities and venues that are assembled in various configurations across these spatially located social milieu.

In this urban nation, this city state, Hood jumps scales. This extension of Hood in its efforts to localize social relations by emphasizing live music performed by and for Singaporeans, creates a "space of engagement" in a hierarchy of scales, political and otherwise that make such engagements possible. In this way the "new Hood" offers alternative urban space in a music scene in which foreign workers dominate the hospitality industry jobs and live music experiences (mostly Filipino musicians are employed in these roles) and international acts dominate the larger, commercial music scene in which Singaporeans pay ticket prices to see perfomances in large-capacity concert halls and venues. The consequences have had effect on the spatio-sonic scale that was the old Hood. The possibility for masculine displays as central to the vibrancy of the space is limited, diminished by increasing scale itself. Yet the space of engagement still exists, it's still possible. It's just another alternative in a sonic democracy.

This change in location is considered here as "jumping scales." Rather than explore the capital involved in the capacity to jump scale in urban commercial settings for the augmentation of economic conditions, this chapter, from an ethnographic perspective, observes the effect on the community of friends who have participated in both assemblages. Alternative urban space in this case is re-assembled again and again not only from interest but from a habitus deeply local and fiercely Singaporean – and so broadly alternative – in spite of the transformation of the live performance experience from one "space of engagement" to another.

In 2013, Hood changed locations – jumping scale as Harvey might say for purposes of capital, and he wouldn't be wrong. In the case presented here of "jumping" spatio-sonic scales from shophouse to mall, extending the "reach" in the assemblage of networks also extended affective possibilities. Across these "spaces of engagement" and in spite of radical changes to live music format and technique, range of musical genre, food and beverages, spatial size, location, staff, and so forth, this community of musicians and friends continues to patronize the pub as a particularly Singaporean place, but moreover as place to nurture and to assemble a particularly Singaporean sonically charged way of "apprehending" their world. In a city state intent on tight control over the presence of spatio-sonic scales (by way of the Public Entertainments Act), ethnographic attention to a local pub featuring live music encounters a vernacular community and popular culture made by Singaporeans for themselves.

"These are atypical Singaporeans"

"These are atypical Singaporeans," the stranger standing next me said as we gulped down glasses of whiskey with belinjau chips. "This whole thing is not usual here," he continued, "These are noisy people."[45] This conversation was taking place among a group of Singaporeans, 20 or so, gathered together for food and drink in celebration of the final day of Chinese New Year. The gathering point was located in the basement of an aging mall in Singapore's

central business district. At the dead-end of a hallway, across the hall from a
drum studio is a diminutive storefront attached to a storeroom affectionately
referred to as "the Doghouse."

Figure 23. The Doghouse. Almost ready for jam time. Photo by author, 2015.

Named as the habitat of its proprietor, a rock and blues musician who was a
founder of the 1960s legendary psychedelic band known as The Straydogs, the
Doghouse is the occasional home to a small community of amateur and semi-
professional musicians, their family members, friends, and fans. Complete with
makeshift bar, guitars, guitar amplifiers, and a few chairs, the Doghouse hosts
this group on Mondays and Fridays for happy hour jams at the end of the work
day. The group, which mostly consists of men, congregates until early evening
hours to play music (jam), drink, smoke, eat, and make a little trouble in this
out-of-the-way place, deep in the basement of this bargain mall known for its
overwhelmingly "Burmese" clientele. In fact the Peninsular Shopping Centre is
known as "Little Burma," providing services, food, and shopping to Singapore's
Myanmar community

The Doghouse is a relative of Guitar 77, Kiang's guitar shop that recently
closed. It is named after its Straydog proprietor, and hosts, as did Guitar 77,

happy hour jam sessions every Monday and Friday beginning around 6 pm. Guitar 77 jam sessions were well known in this basement crossroads, and were tolerated rather than celebrated by neighboring stores. The time of day helped foster tolerance as many of the tailors, massage parlours, used electronics shops, and CD stores close for the day by the time the sessions begin. Noise and temporality are symbiotic in this case, and the same symbiosis is crucial for the Doghouse sessions as well. But if you make your way to this subterranean sonic marketplace when sessions are ongoing, the noise is unmistakable, and can be heard emanating from a corridor that must be found in order to determine the origin of the often explosive sounds of blues and rock music played at high volume levels and significantly distorted for the listening pleasure of those Doghouse participants who frequent these weekly sonic gatherings. The participants in the Guitar 77 sessions and now those that take place at the Doghouse are a group of men of various ages and backgrounds.

Figure 24. Warming up the gear in The Doghouse. Photo by author, 2015.

Class is not a defining feature, although most of the men are working men. Salesmen, shipping-container brokers, schoolteachers, investment bankers, retail sales personnel, retirees, the un- and under-employed, and even professors represent a small sample of the occupations of those present at any one session. Ethnic and religious backgrounds vary as well, although most of the men are

Chinese Singaporeans, and most would say they are Christians to varying degrees. Young and old alike can show up, and they do. The sessions are lively, and sonics are always accompanied by copious amounts of alcohol and finger foods purchased from stalls and restaurants nearby, or gastronomic contributions picked up by participants on the way from work.

There is no need for participants to bring their own gear – guitars and amplifiers are onsite to play. The gear available to play is not the best of the best as can be found in the other shops. Mostly cobbled together, homemade, and repaired guitars and amplifiers are available to play, even though in the storeroom some of the finest guitars and amplifiers currently available for retail sale are at hand. Participants plug into 1970s Ibanez tube screamer distortion pedals, Fender Twin Reverb amplifiers, and other old-school gear, jamming to a musical genre equally old-school, whether rock classics like Jimi Hendrix's "Little Wing," AC/DC, or Van Halen. At times, players jam to more contemporary tunes, but for the most part rock and roll classics dominate. Volume levels are generally high as most players attempt to reach orgasmic climaxes sonically achieved with each tune and with varying degrees of skill. In fact, this is the sonic structure for each jam. False starts and stopping mid-stream are common, and disrupt flow. Sonic completions are celebrated with applause and exclamations of "Wah!" Listening is accompanied by conversation, drinking, and eating. No one is expected to sit down and listen only.

The Doghouse jam sessions share forms of performativity with onstage jams and performances in Singapore. While onstage during our first performance in 2012 as Blues 77, Kiang approached the microphone just as we finished the first song of our set and announced to the crowd, "Everyone here is talking cock." In fact, Kiang often took onstage opportunities to remind the crowd that the performance that included us, the music, the audience, the amplified sonics, the alcohol, the smoking, the intoxication, the loud boisterous crowd calls and responses, the contained spatio-sonic scale threatening to sonorously escape all limits physical or otherwise, all contributed to the noisy affair as "taking cock." After the guitar shop was closed down these "garrulous affairs of power" were sensed again – reproduced – in the Doghouse with differing degrees of sonic and experiential intensity.

Assembled over and over again, these Doghouse talking cock sessions are composed as personal, yet at the same time as collective cultural festivals of masculine performativity. The "rocker" or rock and roll lifestyle is the social category celebrated at these events. Kiang, of course, embodies this social category authentically. He himself is lived heritage and embodies the rock and roll cosmopolitanism celebrated at these events. In the Doghouse, stored away safely in a battered green guitar case, is the group totem: an early 1970s white-aging-to-cream Fender Stratocaster guitar, once owned by legendary Singaporean guitarist, also former Straydog, Jimmy Appadurai. The guitar is a material embodiment and extends the cosmopolitanism celebrated during the jam sessions. The guitar has been signed by every person who has been an official member of the band across the years. I am proud to say the guitar features my signature. There is talk of donating the guitar to a museum, or selling it for outrageous amounts of money because of its aura, its history, its significance to Straydog history and the history of rock and roll in Singapore. This multiply inflected heritage embodied in the guitar, a heritage that includes personal and national histories in one of the most iconic rock images and material objects – a white Stratocaster guitar – centers the energy of this community of musicians and friends. Kiang never has to bring the guitar out of the case; it sits locked up in a corner of the storeroom. On occasion the guitar is put on display as friends arrive for afternoon drinking and jamming. Everyone knows it's there whether we see it or not. The material presence of the guitar signifies in spite of the fact that it remains mostly stored away.

Figure 25. Kiang, The Doghouse host. Photo by author, 2015.

Figure 26. The Fender Stratocaster signed by all members of The Straydogs. The Doghouse totem. Photo by author, 2015.

The social that emerges around the afternoon happy hour jam sessions connects with cosmopolitan sonic history as a way of thinking and feeling embodied in the guitar; a way of thinking and feeling, as Feld (2012) might say, an acoustemology organized around a "convivial cosmopolitanism" (Mignolo 2000) anchored simultaneously in both history and the present. While this local community of interests and of place are clearly assembled and re-assembled self-consciously among friends and family, the fluid, permeable, open-ended nature of this group means that on any day, at any time, anyone, especially if that someone can recognize the not entirely nor always coherent "cultural biography" embodied and projected in things and by the activities in the store – drinking, the blues, guitars, men talking cock, jamming, heritage – can join in. Singaporeans of several generations and non-Singaporeans are welcome, as in my case.

This small community in a vernacular milieu of the Doghouse endures with each new actualization, each new representation of itself and so performs memorably. As Attali (2009: 8) argues, "any organization of sounds" is "equivalent to the articulation of a space," indexing "the limits of a territory" and a "refuge for residual irrationality." Like the Fender guitar made in America, the cultural biographies of the rocker way of thinking and knowing, and at times being in the world become quintessentially Singaporean: a raucous noisy fiercely Singaporean cosmopolitanism sonically expressed in the Monday and Friday jam sessions where men can talk cock, drink, smoke, behave as atypical Singaporeans for a few hours in a space off to the side of the proverbial road, out of the way of the mainstream.[46]

Figure 27. Cosmopolitan conviviality at The Doghouse. Photo by author, 2015.

The group is assembled and adheres through related reciprocal exchanges that are central to the fashioning of this cosmopolitanism. One can exchange and so engage in cosmopolitan conviviality sonically – playing guitars, drums, singing, shared and unique experiences told as stories, simply showing up and being present, adding one's voice to the sonics of these afternoon jam sessions. Reciprocity also involves things – alcohol, cigarettes, band gear, food, and other appropriate items of consumption that may add to the after work time affairs that take place now in this even more out-of-the-way space in the basement of the mall. Those who travel outside of Singapore for business or pleasure are expected to use their duty-free limits on alcohol purchases as they make their way through the airport. These bottles of alcohol, mostly whiskey and scotch, are contributed to the jam sessions.

Significant exchanges, however, involve the songs themselves and the time involved in jamming the songs. Songs everyone knows carry great value as methexic rather than mimetic vehicles for action, in that well-known songs help move the action and the community. Even though players may try to copy the chord changes and solos as they are sounded on recordings, the texts that inform jamming as an "instrument of understanding" among participants, "mutations are audible" and expected (Attali 2009: 4). These opportunities to mimic and mutate hold great sonic, and so community, value. As well, the time involved as each participant is given a chance to jam, a chance to play music, is reciprocal as well. Monopolizing jam time, for example, playing too many songs, or taking up too much of the solo opportunities can spoil the flow of events. In either case, whether participants play well-known or obscure musics, play too long and too much, tolerance is the most valuable characteristic of all in the doghouse regime of value. To exchange tolerance is to perform "ritual murder," to sacrifice oneself for the collective is proof of membership in the group. In this way the sonics of the Doghouse sessions reach depth as deep sound.

Community membership and fun are measured by the flow in the event and by these exchanges. Huizinga long ago noted the centrality of "fun" in the flow of play. The noisy happy hours are play: significant events actualizing rule-bound, non-ordinary realities, temporally and sequentially emplaced in which participants are absorbed in the suspension of normal life (Huizinga 1950). As Geertz (1973) found in the deep play of the Balinese cockfight, in these talking cock sessions reciprocal exchange is fundamental to the rules of membership that evoke masculine forms of conviviality: sonically charged, spatially organized, masculine cosmopolitan festivals of flow and fun, made more so by the reciprocal exchanges small and large, deep and shallow as Geertz would note.

And so in this noisy mall, where Little Burma resides specially and spatially alongside tattoo parlors, used camera shops, cheap clothing, shoe stores, and guitar shops, this small community of musicians and friends gather to make noise, and in the process make community. As a spatio-sonic scale the noisy Doghouse activities reach beyond the physical spatial limits designated by the location in this out-of-the-way corner of a basement in a mall. The reach of the noise attracts attention, engaging in a "politics of noise" (Donald 2011). The reciprocal exchanges also attract attention and similarly hold the potential for reach beyond the event as the potential for enduring relations forged through obligation are socially reproduced beyond the Doghouse space. This capacity to attract attention on the various levels, involving various scales increases the stakes: as in the deep play of the cockfight, the sound, or the noise, becomes deep (Ferzacca 2012).

Social relations and conduct in such communities as Fox (2004: 30) noted for the honky-tonk bar scene of country music performers and fans are "mediated primarily by ritualized forms of intimate social interaction." Thompson (1993: 530) in his history of the use of "rough music" as a form of social control and cultural critique in 19th-century working-class neighborhoods and villages in England illustrates a way in which such communities of interest in vernacular milieu employ ritualized forms as a "mode of life in which some part of the law belongs still to the community and is theirs to enforce."

The guitar shops, the basement, the gear, the people, comprise the context in which those who gather for jam sessions at the Doghouse assemble as a "community of interest" within a "vernacular milieu"(Pickering and Green 1987). Pickering and Green, concerned about the "penetration of capital" and so echoing Thompson, Elias, Gramsci, describe the vernacular milieu as:

> ...the local environment and specific immediate contexts within which, as an integral part of their everyday life, people participate in non-mediated forms and processes of cultural life. By definition that cultural life is non-official and while it is at times assimilated into the national culture it is experientially felt and understood by its participants as quite distinct (ibid. p.2).

The music business, and so the penetration of capital is essential to the network of things and people that assemble on Monday and Friday evenings at the Doghouse in the monument to bargain shopping. In fact, the mall as a crossroads of local and global things and people charges the gatherings at the Doghouse in specific, even ritualized ways in spite of the central presence of business and music capitalism. Music capitalism provides the cover for the jam sessions held at the Doghouse, as such activities border on the fringes of illegality. As a guitar shop, jam sessions are disguised as business affairs rather than merely drinking, eating, socializing, and playing loud music in a public space. Thus, for the vernacular milieu in this case the penetration of capital is crucial and operates as a cover tune – a familiar and recognizable sonic expression that represents and also disguises the affairs at hand. Without the other guitar shops and without the small storefront, these activities would not be allowed by state authorities to occur. Mall security and state managed through zoning and licensing ensure the public safety from such noisy disturbances.

The noisy use of public space in the mall, even an out-of-the-way public space can easily be seen and heard as a "device of saturation" in which the social fabric of this small community of musicians and friends in a vernacular milieu is rendered (Foucault 2007: 45). Duffy and Waitt (2013: 472) argue that sonic experience "assembles and re-assembles relationships," in particular "relationships that comprise home." In their considerations, sound and "sonorous assemblages" afford "spatial and temporal experiences" in the making sense of self and social identities in the performativity of social practices" (ibid., p. 472). In the Doghouse, Kiang and our friends reconfigure and re-sound the spatiality and temporality of a vernacular community as a noisy, sonorous assemblage anchored in both the past and present network of relations.

However, while participation and membership in this community is validated by the noise and noisy activity in sensuous terms as a call to the human feeling of community, as an intensification in local experience in a vernacular milieu, the vital organization of the state effect is ever-present – present as Kong (2006) illustrates for popular music in Singapore through "both discursive and legislative acts." In fact, the presence of the state, its heritage, and participation in past "moral panics" that help define the noise at play is crucial to the spirit of the community (ibid.). Legislation directed at limiting public performances, the use of noise in public space, and the possession and consumption of alcohol threaten participation in Doghouse activities. In this specific case, the real estate rates and rental policies of this mall and shopping centre play a central role in containing "the performative aspects of music embodying the sensual and the violent" (ibid., p. 103). The state and past moral panics haunt and so afford the normative social roles that in this case perform as noisy social identities and practices. In this way Doghouse images, activities, and associations assembled among networks of human and non-human forces present, or afford "spaces of dependence."

Sonic parameters and tolerances translated into spatial dimensions and proximities depending upon the prevailing allocations of designations at any one time constitute an ontology for "spaces of dependence" organized as state sponsored urban and social planning in a "politics of scale" in which sound is a crucial determining feature.[47] Recently Kelvin Low, Jim Sykes and others have explored "the spatial politics of noise" in this "city state." Their work highlights the role of the state in urban affairs of life through legislative and licensing procedures that manage social conflicts between different kinds of sonic activities through the organization of socio-spatial presences as well as absences.[48] The local live music scene in Singapore assembles within state "reach" as spatio-sonic scales, the durations of which are responses to access to public space for live music performances on one hand and the difficulties of establishing, maintaining, and sustaining a live music venue in a challenging business environment on the other. These "spaces of engagement" are crucial sites "in which the politics of securing a space of dependence unfolds" (Cox 1998: 2).

As one observer recently pointed out, "noisy people" in Singapore need their own "playgrounds."[49] The Doghouse is actualized as one of these playgrounds, a space of engagement that as a vernacular milieu celebrates the "rocker" and the rock and roll lifestyle as it existed and is configured in both the past and present. Unlike the "soft power" of the cultural industries in the region as forms of "cultural diplomacy... influencing the opinions and attitudes of transnational audiences," (Chua 2012: 119 & 121) the Doghouse assemblages are poorly positioned to shift audience perceptions, but rather are well positioned to celebrate a cosmopolitan conviviality anchored in heritage and present, and in local experience. It is the centrality of this cosmopolitanism embodied in 1960s rock and roll images, activities, and associations reproduced presently in local experience that becomes a focus for alternative forms of interaction and identity formation.[50] It is this troubling of the state effect and discursive projects of self and person in Singapore that the particular activities described here intend to explore.[51]

The images, activities, and associations that are the Doghouse as community verge on the cusp of legality, in fact, some of what goes on could lead to charges. The community bar, the smoking, the use of public space for musical performance are all illegal activities literally and figuratively speaking. The out-of-the-way location protects the community to some extent. But the noise draws curious others who make their way to the Doghouse to see what all the noise is about. Drum students and instructors from a drum studio nearby shuffle past the group quickly without anything being said. Kiang and his fun time are well known by now in this basement, and so are tolerated. Complaints are infrequent. Nevertheless, this space of dependence haunts and so charges the activities and images that are composed during the afternoon Doghouse sessions with meanings of alternative ways of knowing, feeling, and being in the world.

The emphasis on reciprocal exchange and the irrationality of economic values involved are sonic expressions of a political economy at odds with the rational, development state that is Singapore. In fact, the Doghouse exists as a mirror image of Kiang's "business model" that favors gift logic approach to life that appears counter to the hegemony best business practices that emphasize economic profit and gain. He often attributes his ups and downs in life to his unsound business practices.

And while the Doghouse houses atypical Singaporeans and others involved in atypical Singaporean activities, being and behaving as noisy people in an out-of-the-way playground are not the only troubling characteristics of Kiang and his group of friends. The Doghouse sessions create memories, and it is this creative potential and actualization that trouble conventional images of typical

Singaporeans. The state effect, embodied in these spatio-sonic engagements is ever present. And so some noisy people have, for now, found a playground their urban dreams and aspirations are imagined and realized.

Chapter Four

Sonic Circuits

Touring Sonic Circuits

Kiang tells a story of the time in the mid 1960s when The Straydogs were offered the opportunity to travel to Saigon, South Vietnam, to perform. It was the heady days of the American Vietnam War and since he was a minor, 16 years of age at the time, he needed his father's permission in the form of a signature in order to obtain a passport to travel. When he asked his father, The Chief, to sign the permission letter, his father responded to his request with a slap to his face. Kiang was becoming a bit of a disappointment to his father – his mother by this time had already passed away. Kiang had no interest in school and had failed most of his exams that would track him if he had continued on past primary school. Kiang remembers that back then all he wanted to do was become a "rockstar." As school related failures mounted, his father at one time had young Kiang kneel down with bare knees on conch shells while his father caned him. The courage to ask for permission to travel to Saigon came from friends who were making the trip – friends who did not go on to become The Straydogs, but friends who were members of other Singaporean bands recruited to entertain along the sonic circuits that were emerging with English-language popular music at this time in the region.

In the 1960s in Singapore and other urban centres in Southeast Asia, global popular music, also originating in cities in Europe and North America helped produce a "vibrant and creative period" in Southeast Asian musical and cultural history (Adil 2014). The rock and popular music resounded and resonated with the ruptures of post-colonial nation-building and war in the region. The lyrics to The Straydogs' EMI recorded single "Freedom" embodies the sense of the times not only in Singapore but around the world:

> Close your eyes, let times fly
> Take a trip the time is nigh
> Arm yourself with freedom rights
> Were gonna touch the sky[52]

97

The music, like the times, simultaneously offered cosmopolitan fun and danger. Ethno-nationalists feared the damaging influences of western popular culture on the peoples, particularly the youth, of these newly emerging nation-state societies. Bell-bottoms, miniskirts, and long hair were on the one hand "good clean fun," but on the other hand "subversive youth trends" reflected the threatening and dangerous presence of "yellow culture" – a pornographic, obscene influence embodied in the "beat music of English-language bands" (Adil 2014: 136–137).[53] While local Southeast Asian bands playing the songs and sounds of popular music from Europe and North America "demonstrated" to local Southeast Asians that loving music was not only fun, but potentially an opportunity to be "creative and successful" (Thom 2014: 131), the "hippism" associated with the music, the unshaven facial hair, long hair, and brawls that broke out at local performances led to "youth harassment and banning of musical performances" (Adil 2014: 136).[54]

The tea dances in Singapore held at the Orchard Hotel and on the military bases featuring Singaporean musicians playing "western pop music" current at the time were devices of urban saturation for military personnel and Southeast Asians alike. Southeast Asian musicians traveled to R & R cities to take advantage of emerging sonic opportunities just as "authentic" and "indigenous cultural forms" had long trafficked colonial and imperial sonic circuits prior to the end of colonialism and emergence of the nation states in the region. These sonicities, that attended to the needs of military service personnel and foreign performance spaces in the Southeast Asian region, were generally denigrated by the region's leaders at the time (Noslzlopy & Cohen 2010).

Kiang and his band wanted to go to Saigon to play the beats and blues music they were becoming known for in Singapore. Saigon, as a wartime urban center, attracted bands playing English-language popular music. In addition to attracting musicians, audiences traveled along wartime R & R circuits circulating foreign military personnel around the region. Similar to the centrifugal, centripetal capacities of inland Southeast Asian galactic polities and coastal trading port cities in the past, colonial cities and emergent urban centres in the rapidly approaching post-colonial era afforded opportunities for sonic circuits to develop – musical circuits of mobile sound providing a sense of home for some and cosmopolitan modernity for others in addition to leisure, rest, recuperation, and income.

After enduring the slap to his face, Kiang listened as his father explained that if he went off to Saigon his son would surely return a drug addict; a "heroin addict" more specifically. Now Kiang believes his father knew best. He says his friends came back "fucked up" and all of them have since "died." He ended his story by celebrating with a great sense of pride his filial devotion to his father in later life, after his other brothers and sisters had moved on with their own lives, leaving The Chief and his failing fortunes for someone else to pay attention to. Kiang ends his story with a smile as he tells of the care he continued to provide to a man who had attempted, sometimes brutally, to control teenage passions for the cosmopolitan feast that was rock and roll.

Singapore music historian, Joseph Pereira, documents that tea dances in Singapore beginning in the early 1960s and later banned on New Year's Day 1970, drew "servicemen" stationed in Singapore and around the region for "beats and blues" sessions held at basement clubs like the Golden Venus located on Orchard Road (Pereira 2011). In designated R & R cities like Singapore, popular GI clubs appeared as significant Southeast Asian venues for local musicians to practice and perform English-language popular music leading to a wide range of well-rehearsed bands playing covers as well as original music (Pereira 1999). Joseph Tham (2014: 130) notes that the popularity of these bands among service personnel led to opportunities to perform "overseas." Singaporean bands competed with "Filipino bands" as a "call went out all over Asia" for English-language popular music to entertain the troops, particularly in the wartime region of Vietnam (Pereira 2011: 17). USO tours recruited Singaporean bands to play shows in South Vietnam (Pereira 1999: 8). Radio broadcast English-language popular music for the troops. Some Southeast Asian musicians and bands formed bands organizing set lists and repertoire around the hits of the day.[55] The appetite for English-language popular music was nurtured by these participants in Singapore's emerging music scene both at home and on the road, producing an "increased mobility of musicians" in the 1960s that was "part of a more general process of cosmopolitanism and exchange" (Agustin and Lockhead 2015: 162).

Veronica Young, a 1960s pop singer in Singapore, sometimes billed as the "Connie Francis of Southeast Asia" told me about her experiences in the R & R circuit during the Vietnam War years in Southeast Asia. Sitting together backstage after a show at Singapore's Esplanade Concert Hall, I first heard of her travels to Saigon.[56] Later in a Facebook message Veronica remarked:

> Yes Steve I was there twice each time a contract of 4 months. U.S. Dollars were 1 to 4 so a lot of entertainers were picked by agents to perform and I poke my nose in it and it was a great experience. Will tell you all in details one day when I come visit you ha ha if offers still stand.[57]

Other cities in the region provided R & R destinations: Kuala Lumpur and Penang in Malaysia, Manila in the Philippines, and Bangkok in Thailand, were officially sanctioned cities for rest and recuperation by the American military for soldiers fighting the war (Hawai'i, Sydney, Hong Kong, Taipei, and Tokyo rounded out the official list). Soldiers often preferred to visit cities located in Southeast Asia because it meant less time wasted on travel, and therefore more precious R & R time to drink, party, shop, enjoy female companionships, meet with family (usually wives), and upgrade military hardware as well as sightseeing and so forth. As has been illustrated, finding familiar music was also a desired R & R activity. These sonic circuits, in which local musicians became exposed to and performed popular music from the core states of North America and Europe, are the early sources of exposure to cosmopolitan musics for Singaporeans and other Southeast Asians at the time.

Over the four years from 2012 to 2016, I followed a band from Singapore on trips to perform in Ho Chi Minh City, Vietnam – formerly Saigon – and Melaka, Malaysia. Following the same sonic circuits that appeared during the late 1960s, these "boys' trips" embraced many of the same images, activities, and associations involved in those 20th-century wartime music tours that Kiang so desperately wanted to experience when he was a teenager.

Figure 28. Boy's trip. At Changi Airport, Singapore, headed to Ho Chi Minh City, Vietnam, for a gig. Photo by author, 2013.

While those tours were made during a period of violence and nation-building occurring throughout Southeast Asia, the contemporary boys' trips occur in the era of broadly available mobility fostered among the nations of this region. A group of men "playing the blues," all aged over 60 may seem an odd fit in this bustling Southeast Asian city. However, men from Southeast Asia and beyond traveling to participate in regional and global commerce as well as the delights of the cosmopolitan urban enclaves of this region are nothing new. Such trading port cities have always accommodated odd fits not unlike this motley crew of Singaporean men who fancy themselves as a blues band. Myself, a 62-year-old anthropologist and band member (guitar, vocals) in addition to Kiang, a 66-year-old retired music store owner and bass player, and James a 67-year-old successful shipping-container broker and drummer formed a band in 2011 known as Blues 77. After numerous jam sessions in Kiang's store when it was still open for business, we decided to perform as a band in local pubs in Singapore featuring live music. The enthusiastic response to our music encouraged us to continue to perform, and before long I found I was participating in fieldwork and a new project as an anthropologist engaged in what I refer to as sonic ethnography.

Figure 29. Placard for the gig in Ho Chi Minh City. Photo by author, 2013.

Various infrastructural developments facilitate Southeast Asian mobilities for increasing numbers of Southeast Asians who now have opportunities to travel the region like never before. These boys' trips are conversant with and embody much of the content of the R & R sonic circuits of the past. However, in the case of this small community of musicians, family, and friends, traveling these sonic circuits in this time of Southeast Asian mobility, selective localization, a social and cultural feature of the longue durée of mobility in Southeast Asian history travels (Watson-Andaya 1997). This capacity of Southeast Asians to forge locally significant assemblages from historical, cultural, political, economic, and social currents that course through this crossroads to the world is, in the case of these boys' trips, portable and productive in similar ways to the emplaced versions of selective localization characteristic of the cultural history of the region.

Figure 30. Ho Chi Minh City from the rooftop. Photo by author, 2013.

A particular imaginary of Singaporean urbanity, one that is generational and masculine, is selectively localized as the boys travel. Familial, specifically fraternal, relations reflective of the region but also in particular social life in Singapore are re-localized. The spirit of cosmopolitanism and masculine conviviality celebrated by this group of men sonically, reproduced as beats and blues music, accompanies the boys on these trips. Nostalgia specific to Singapore provides significant comparison in local renderings of other urban spaces. Finally, bodily practices and body work mark the circular mobility involved as the return to Singapore is anticipated in every image, every association, and every activity involved in these portable selection localizations that follow the sonic channels that have charged the personal histories of those involved. The "micro geographies of everyday life" (Cresswell, 2011, 551) that are contained in these sonic circuits evoke "gendered subjectivities, familial and social networks, spatially segregated urban neighborhoods, national images and aspirations to modernity, and global relations" all at once as we travel to make some music (Sheller and Urry 2006: 209).

Infrastructures and Mobilities: Visa Facilitations, Budget Airlines, Mediated Connectivity

Simmel (2001[1903]) suggested the urban demands tempo and precision. Sheller and Urry (2006: 216) remark that currently auto-mobility is a "powerful socio-technical system" that involves the "recentering of the corporeal body as an affective vehicle through which we sense place and movement, and construct emotional geographies." Finally Pellegrino (2012) illustrates that "non-transport information networks" facilitate or suppress mobility. Visa facilitation, low-cost airfares, rapid economic growth, increasing urbanization in the region, and a swelling middle class have contributed to the increasing demand for regional travel in Southeast Asia (Brandon 2014).

In 1967, the Association for Southeast Asian Nations, ASEAN, was formed primarily for security and political purposes. In recent decades ASEAN countries have moved towards greater regional integration, first in the liberalization of goods and commodity movements across ASEAN borders, and, in 2002 with the ASEAN Tourism Agreement summit in Phnom Penh, the liberalization of transport and tourism invigorating intra-ASEAN circulations and movements among Southeast Asians. The effect of Open Sky Policies for regional tourism cannot be overstated. Pushing such policies and agreements has been the "growing activity of budget airlines in Asia" changing the contour and magnitude of regional tourism (Servino 2006: 240).

Visa facilitation programs in the region reduce and streamline applications and fees associated with travel visas. At the time of the agreement, many ASEAN nations already had in place "visa-free arrangements" for ASEAN nationals.

However, the agreement waives visa requirements and travel taxes for travelers who are citizens of the 10 member nations (Myanmar has yet to institute these policies). One measure of the effect of visa facilitation policies in the region on the movements and mobility of ASEAN citizens is reflected in numbers of tourists requiring visas for entry into Southeast Asian countries. In 2013, of the 89 million "tourists" who travelled the region, only 10 percent needed to obtain a "traditional visa."[58]

The budget airline market in Southeast Asia has experienced massive, dramatic growth since 2000. Malaysia's AirAsia has rapidly expanded to become the major carrier in the region, operating right across the subcontinent and opening up the possibility of flying to many Asians who previously would never have considered it due to the cost. Since then a number of competitors, including Singapore's Tiger Airways and Australia's Qantas-owned Jetstar, have emerged in the regional airline market along with a growing number of others. While multi-lateral "open sky" agreements remain on the ASEAN table, the "liberalization" of airspace in the region continues (Eason 2012). Bloomsburg reports there are now 47 budget airlines in the Asia-Pacific region, with a combined fleet of a 1,000 aircraft. An additional 1,500 planes are on order. In 2013, Southeast Asian budget airlines captured 30 percent of the region's market for air travel. Singapore, where low-fare carriers hold more than five times that share of the air travel market compared to low-cost carriers in North Asia for example, remains a central hub, a significant crossroads for cheap air travel in ASEAN as well as for non-regional travelers moving around the region's airspace (Wang and Lee 2014).

The online presence of this market and the ability to access the market through handphones and computers is the modus operandi for organizing our tours of sonic circuits throughout the region. From 1998 to 2003, internet users in Asia rose from 24.4 million users to 137 million; a growth rate of 561 percent (Eid and Hughes 2013). In Singapore alone during the same period internet users increased 312 percent from 0.6 million to 1.9 million (ibid.). In response to this fast-paced, increasing market demand brought about by internet access and usage, many airlines and travel agencies have been working hard to develop their own websites to facilitate e-commerce transactions. Nowadays, most airline and travel websites are designed to provide one-stop service. They are not only informative, but also functional, allowing internet users to book a flight online, make hotel and car reservations, register for package tours, and carry out other key functions. Visa facilitation and low-cost airfares reflect and influence the rapid economic growth, increasing urbanization in the region, and a swelling middle class that many experts attribute to the increasing demand for air travel.

Figure 31. Boys' Trip to Bui Vien Street, Ho Chi Minh City. Photo by author, 2013.

Nearly everyone who participates in this small community of musicians and friends is very active online and in growing e-commerce channels. Traveling in and around the region using budget airlines, taking advantage of visa facilitations, and managing this travel online is a frequent occurrence among members of this group. Bangkok, Ho Chi Minh City, Yangon, Chiang Mai, Melaka, Kuala Lumpur, Penang, and Jakarta, are favored destinations, mostly for leisure, but at times for business as well. Beaches and nature eco-tours are not an attraction – travel is mostly between urban centers, and urbanities are the appeal in contrast to a desire to interact with "nature." The standard features of any place deemed visitation-worthy is whether or not there are bars, pubs, and readily available alcohol, and whether or not there is some kind of nightlife with "great food." Speaking with band members before a trip, one of the younger musicians inquired as to the availability of bars and alcohol, stating that this was a necessary requirement for his participation. This sensuous urbanity allows for the potential for equally "sensuous conduct."[59] In fact, I can't imagine any of these boys' trips to be anything but urban adventures.

All of this is managed in Singapore and on location using social media, made available through smart phones. Facebook and WhatsApp are favored.

The availability of Wi-Fi in urban settings makes these media appealing. The use of social media in combination with available Wi-Fi is an easier and less costly method of contact compared to the use of cellular networks.[60] The management of travel arrangements, the scheduling of performances, the coordination of the social relations and activities involved, all facilitated by handphone and computer, reflect the urban demands for tempo and precision Simmel recognized for late 19th-century and early 20th-century urbanisms. For example a selection from a WhatApp group chat illustrates the timing and precision involved in the arrangements for the trip as it unfolds:

1/14/16, 7:12:46 PM: I arrive hotel around 530 pm.
1/14/16, 7:13:58 PM: My itinerary is same as -----. Who else is traveling with
                        us the same time?
1/14/16, 7:21:06 PM: See you at the airport tomorrow -----
1/14/16, 7:35:36 PM: ----..meet at 5.30.
1/14/16, 7:35:45 PM: Okie
1/14/16, 7:35:55 PM:[thumbs up emoji]
1/14/16, 7:42:35 PM: Ok -----.
1/14/16, 9:06:03 PM: I'm leaving Sg at 1pm. Are you at that time also?
1/14/16, 9:06:44 PM: Nope. My timing is 4 pm.
1/14/16, 9:07:03 PM: Ok.
1/14/16, 9:07:15 PM: Shit I think I'm alone after all....
1/14/16, 9:07:55 PM: I'm. Leaving sg 720am
1/14/16, 9:09:27 PM: Me too.
1/14/16, 9:09:36 PM: Tiger
1/14/16, 9:10:01 PM: Huh?
1/14/16, 9:10:29 PM: I'm leaving Vietnam on Monday 9:20am flight.
1/14/16, 9:10:42 PM: Anyone on that timing?
1/14/16, 9:11:52 PM: Me.
1/15/16, 12:20:20 AM: Hey ----- breakfast tomorrow? 7?
1/15/16, 12:27:04 AM: Yes breakfast at 7
1/15/16, 9:17:16 AM: what room am I allocated?
1/15/16, 9:49:32 AM: where's my airport pick up?
1/15/16, 9:50:06 AM: What is the address of the hotel?
1/15/16, 9:50:26 AM: [address]
1/15/16, 9:50:44 AM: [address]

This automobility combines the social and the technical within compressed time frameworks and precise coordination so that all of us can engage in the same experience – the same sense of place and movement in order to construct emotional geographies transported from Singapore to locations along sonic circuits in the region, in this case Melaka and Ho Chi Minh City. As information networks facilitate mobility, boys' trips generate the re-centering of bodies so that habits and desires reflecting those established and long-nurtured in Singapore are selectively localized in another urban milieu. Infrastructure as tempo, in this case the compression of time embodied in visa facilitations and flights, and as precision, embodied in the management and coordination of activities through scheduling and online arrangements constitutes a mediated connectivity between places and among social relations that facilitate the selective localization of Singaporean values and sensibilities in other places. What are these specific values and sensibilities selectively re-localized in the experience of these boys trips that travel sonic circuits in order to have fun?

Figure 32. Fun on the road. Ho Chi Minh City. Photo by author, 2013.

"Boys Trips": Selective Sensibilities in Motion

We arrived at Ho Chi Minh City airport fully loaded with guitars, whiskey, Vietnamese dong, and an entourage of fellow Singaporeans who came along as an audience and for some "fun." This was our second trip to perform in this southern Vietnamese city as the Singaporean blues band known as Blues 77.[61] Besides "gigs" in Singapore, we had performed in Melaka, Malaysia, as well, following in the tracks of long established mobilities relevant with the appearance of Southeast Asian Straits Settlements and trading port cities. We previously played Ho Chi Minh to an audience of Vietnamese at the Rock Fan Club[62] located near the Independence Palace, the former American consulate, an iconic symbol of the North Vietnamese victory over the South and the Americans in 1975. This time we were performing at Saigon Ranger, a club located downtown catering mostly to the expats that litter this city of 10 million people and 7 million motorbikes.

There is some difficulty considering these tours as tourism. The cities themselves, while attractive for various reasons, are not visited so as to see the sites. Nor are these trips professional music tours, although we get paid for our performances from time to time. We don't travel as creative labor, nor do we travel as troubadours, like shining Middle Age knights of poetic fictions, even though we are certainly a group of men telling stories of sorts on the road. Even though we do not have complete control over the mobile mission, we are certainly not traveling as a social category in some care chain. Our mobility is circular, with lives in Singapore that await us while we are away, at least to some extent. In fact what travels is Singapore, and, in this way, the trips can be characterized in part as pilgrimages: travel that encourages people to move literally and metaphorically from their normal, everyday lives. However, I'm arguing, that unlike a pilgrimage, selective localization leads participants away from the common goal of most pilgrims: entrance into, however temporarily, different social and spiritual worlds.

Similar to pilgrimages, and the most important feature of these trips along sonic circuits, is the celebration of Singaporean identity in communion, a personal and social experience referred to in the scholarly literature on the social effect of ritual and pilgrimage as communitas. Communitas is a spontaneous sensation of mutual experience and communication – an effervescence that arises in a group of people particularly during ritual, but in other social contexts as well, denoting experience that transcends the everyday fault lines of social structure. In such situated identity formations class, status, any of the quotidian markers that distinguish everyday lives are suspended as "fellow feeling" becomes present. As in rites of passage, the aftermath of such an experience can be personal and social renewal, even transformation in both self and personhood. For these boys' trips, renewal of Singaporean senses of self and person are more or less for participants as Singaporean men, even though a small number of Singaporean women are often present as participants as well.

Figure 33. Blues 77 performing at the RFC Club, Ho Chi Minh City. Photo by author, 2013.

The local term used to express the presence of communitas is "fun." Experiences and paraphernalia that add to fun are described as "shiok." Generally important elements for fun are urban ones – alcohol, restaurants, live music venues, massage parlors, street food, the experience of bad traffic and dirty streets, all of these elements must in some configuration be available if fun is to be had. The social experience involving such elements of fun determine whether or not these elements in part or as a totality can be described as shiok. There is some concern regarding the quality of urbanity offered on the road in cities other than Singapore. A selection of messages from a WhatsApp group chat for a trip to Ho Chi Minh City reveals some of this concern:

1/14/16, 6:31:01 PM: Hi, we will head for Saigon Ranger after makan to hear some music
1/14/16, 6:31:01 PM: Meet at lobby 6pm
1/14/16, 6:40:10 PM: Hotel room got safe or not? I can't remember
1/14/16, 6:53:47 PM: Got safe sex
1/14/16, 6:54:25 PM: No condoms for sure.

1/14/16, 6:58:02 PM: Ok, just have to stuff my laptop up old man's ass then,
                     if stolen only got one suspect
1/14/16, 6:58:51 PM: No safe

Some Southeast Asian cities are thought to be deficient in terms of these urban
pleasures, for example those in Indonesia, and so do not become desired
destinations. The images, activities, and associations assembled during the
R & R years of these sonic circuits resonate today. R & R cities offering neon-lit
massage parlors, bars and bar girls, modern bathroom facilities, were crucial
elements to the production among servicemen of "mind-boggling experiences"
and "hedonistic binges" difficult to find in rural villages.[63] This similar
relationship to an urban imaginary and to urban practices is central to these
trips along sonic circuits as the central sites are live music venues serving alcohol
if not other modes of obtaining altered consciousness. Another selection from
the group chat illustrates the centrality of such urbanity:

1/15/16, 6:08:57 PM: I'm drinking at a bar opp the hotel. In case anyone wants
                     to join me
1/15/16, 6:09:38 PM: [thumbs up emoji]
1/15/16, 6:10:23 PM: Me and ----- at a restaurant near hotel
1/15/16, 6:11:42 PM: Come join me...beer is cheap here
1/15/16, 6:12:59 PM: Ok
1/15/16, 6:48:43 PM: Is the plan still to meet at the hotel lobby at six, then
                     walk to the market for dinner?
1/15/16, 6:49:36 PM: Ok we will be there
1/15/16, 6:50:20 PM: Yes
1/15/16, 6:50:36 PM: Venue may change
1/15/16, 6:51:21 PM: [thumbs up emoji] See you at the lobby at 6
1/15/16, 6:53:26 PM: Drinking with amateurs
1/15/16, 7:11:27 PM: ----- where you
1/15/16, 7:25:20 PM: I am at a pub on the left of the hotel called champion
1/15/16, 9:27:22 PM: You guys carry on. I'm drinking at Sahara.

Hotel, restaurant, bar, taxi, and airport are anticipated urban places and modes
of urbanity that make the experience fun. Laderman (2009: 17) notes the
growth of urban tourism in the 1950s throughout the region to Vietnam and
other Southeast Asian cities. The prolepsis involved in trafficking these sonic
circuits, especially for the older generation of men who participate in these
trips, is informed by historical imaginaries formed during childhood, during
the 1960s urban cosmopolitan in which they were immersed in Singapore, as

hotels, taxis, bars, clubs and so forth became the signs of the modern urban life of the city.

Figure 34. Gig in Melaka, Malaysia. Photo by author, 2012.

The generational experience involved is not minor. Some of the men are card-carrying Singaporean "pioneers" and the central characters in this group are over 60 years of age. This generational status in the group is marked by kinship terms. "Uncle" is often used by younger men when addressing their elders, but the most common label used is simply "old man."

1/16/16, 11:46:02 AM: Old man where r u?
1/16/16, 11:50:04 AM: Coming up to your room
1/16/16, 11:50:50 AM: I bought shio bak. Any whisky soda?

The older men for the most part run the show. They organize the gigs, arrange the hotel accommodations, accumulate necessary alcohol reserves, and often pay for much of the food and drink that nurture participants along for the trips. In our case Kiang is a central figure in these trips along Southeast Asian sonic circuits and it is his heritage as a 1960s rock musician – a living symbol of that generation of cosmopolitan Singaporeans – that is attractive, operating as a respected status among men old and young. Stories of cosmopolitan Singapore during the 1960s are told, but more important is the narrative, the meta-commentary of Kiang and other old men as the experience unfolds. Old men have the capacity to determine what is shiok or not, and do so as activities take place or are recounted.

This familial communitas complete with fictive kin is a significant feature of the fun that can emerge from these activities. On the boys' trips, there is a fraternal quality to the transactions of relations and forms of association that are assembled. Men participate in body work while on these trips. Group visits to massage parlors, the dentist, and the barber are common activities. Younger men learn to take up these activities from the older men while on the road. While the connections are speculative, there is some plausibility to comparison with the body work involved in R & R circuits in the 1960s, as these men were young in the R & R urban center that was Singapore. Hairstyles and fashion were important features in the lives of Singaporean urban youth during the 1960s, especially those involved with music.[64] The younger men on these trips were generally unaware that less expensive routine dentistry could be a feature of these sonic circuits and accompanied older men to dentists and barbers to attend to body work.

1/16/16, 9:31:41 AM: ------, me ----- and ------ going ... after dentist. Come
                     with us. Lobby 845
1/16/16, 9:31:59 AM: Heading for the market too
1/16/16, 9:32:30 AM: ----- just started w the dentist better make it 9 at the
                     lobby
1/16/16, 9:32:43 AM: Ok 9
1/16/16, 9:33:08 AM: Ok
1/16/16, 9:47:17 AM: Wait for me. I go shower first...

R & R circuits featured "showers, rest, and beer" for war-weary servicemen traveling to a host of Southeast Asian cities during the formative years of the old men in the group (Appy 1993: 237). A prominent image associated with rest and recuperation was massage. Appy (1993: 238) notes the presence in the representations of R & R in magazines, travel brochures, film, and newspapers of "photos of Asian women massaging war-weary GIs." Euphemistically referred to as "steambaths," massage parlors and experiences were urban activities that transformed the R & R that characterized these week-long breaks into "I & I", or intoxication and intercourse (Hickey 2002). Massage is central body work on the sonic junkets, and are organized as group experiences.

1/17/16, 1:19:06 PM: what time go miu?
1/17/16, 1:19:32 PM: Wat is Miu?
1/17/16, 1:19:53 PM: Sleazy massage joint
1/17/16, 1:21:31 PM: I am left with only 800000 and it cost 600000 sorry can't afford
1/17/16, 1:22:20 PM: Go for the barber place?
1/17/16, 1:23:27 PM: I'll pay for your massage la. You pay the sleaze.
1/17/16, 1:25:19 PM: Dinner on me tonight.
1/17/16, 1:26:19 PM: Leaving now?
1/17/16, 1:26:42 PM: Waiting for ----- to reply
1/17/16, 1:27:09 PM: I also short cash leh.
1/17/16, 1:27:17 PM: Aiyah.
1/17/16, 1:27:19 PM: But I prefer the barber
1/17/16, 1:27:33 PM: Is there barber nearby Miu?
1/17/16, 1:27:52 PM: I have the add but it's very xxx
1/17/16, 1:32:23 PM: I had hair wash, ear cleaning, facial scrub and mask for 150k
1/17/16, 1:32:43 PM: No happy ending though.
1/17/16, 1:33:06 PM: Go for hair wash man!

This care for and of bodies taken among the men on these boys' trips, in addition to the eating and drinking, add to the overall sensibility of these sonic experiences as fraternal ones. These activities are also important to the storytelling that continues the experiences once everyone has returned home. Again similar to the stories of R & R exploits, the group returns to Singapore with "tales of blissful indulgence" (Appy 1993: 238). The local ontologies of body workers in sonic destinations such as Ho Chi Minh City, Melaka, Bangkok and so forth that include the masseuse, dentists, barbers, and local dinner guests among others are captured within the circular mobility of the group and it's ontology of male communitas and fraternal modes of care. This selective localization of local ontologies is most clearly evident in the desire for and experiences of intoxication.

1/15/16, 10:04:42 AM: -----: Don't forget the whisky
1/15/16, 10:19:31 AM: I have a bottle for you, the usual
1/17/16, 4:53:23 PM: Let's go to ----- room and do it?
1/17/16, 4:53:40 PM: Is the bottle of whisky with you?
1/17/16, 4:53:56 PM: Later la
1/17/16, 4:54:43 PM: When? 5?
1/17/16, 4:55:26 PM: Yes 5 ok

1/17/16, 4:56:04 PM: Not ready to receive visitors?
1/17/16, 4:56:51 PM: Sleeping
1/17/16, 4:57:32 PM: Sleep old man see you at 5
1/17/16, 5:56:22 PM: I am at lobby
1/17/16, 5:56:55 PM: Where to?
1/17/16, 5:57:13 PM: I'm opp the hotel....having a beer
1/17/16, 5:57:31 PM: Left of the hotel

The attainment of altered states are significant for the boy's trips to be fun and described as shiok. But the altered states have nothing to do with Ho Chi Minh City, Melaka or any of the other sonic destinations except that the resources are available in these localities. The experiences themselves are Singaporean as the modes of expressing intoxication follow talking cock sessions that include boisterous rounds of cheers and loud vocalizing while drinking. At a performance in Ho Chi Minh City at the Saigon Ranger club in 2016, the group stood out among other patrons in the bar for their loudness and exuberance throughout the evening before, during, and after the performance of the band. Likewise the in-room and lobby intoxication sessions are focused group gatherings in which Singapore plays a prominent feature in the conversations that take place. Talking cock is also indulged in during the more private affairs.

Figure 35. Performing in Melaka at Me and Mrs. Jones. Photo by Ana Ferzacca, 2012.

Finally, and especially for the older men, there is a great deal of talk about how cities like Yangon, Ho Chi Minh City, and even Bangkok represent a Singapore of the past, particularly during the 1960s, but in any case a past now left behind as Singapore has developed and become ultra-modern. The dirty streets, the disorderly traffic of automobiles, motorbikes, and persons on the roads and sidewalks, the dismissal of following rules and regulations all hark to a Singapore of old, when Singapore was still kampung. Cheaper prices for food, drink, and generally naughty behavior reflect an embodied adolescence that the older men remember in terms of Singapore's past. Such dirty dangers are precisely the "yellow culture" that Singapore Legislative Debates appearing in the official reports of 1960 set out to eliminate. The Ministry of Culture's campaign against "yellow culture," "blitz" "cinemas, newspapers, magazines and other publishers and distributors disseminating pornographic materials" was the beginning of the regime's blame on colonial rule for Singapore's "cultural devastation," leading to a "crackdown on gambling, prostitution and jukeboxes" in order to create a "distinctive" Singaporean culture "free of the 'westernization' eroding the 'traditional' values of Singapore's presumable 'Eastern' society" (Hong Huang 2008: 87 & 96). In the streets of Ho Chi Minh City, Melaka, Bangkok, Kuala Lumpur, and Phnom Penh, to name a few stops along the sonic circuits of Southeast Asia, this generation of Singaporean men can renew their formative years in these later stages of life in urban milieu and urban practices that remind them of the old days in Singapore. In these ways, the process of selective localization that takes place as an entourage of Singaporeans descends upon various Southeast Asian cities to play music and have "fun" can be considered as portable localizations that generate equally portable local knowledge and identity formation in this time of reduced visa restrictions and budget airfares for ASEAN citizens. These sonic circuits reveal the mobility of selective localizations increasingly becoming a characteristic feature of the region.

Chapter Five

Heritage

Figure 36. Promotional photo for The Straydogs, 1960s. Photo by author, 2017.

Since the 1990s, the heritage movement has gained attention and a deep foothold in Singapore. Government and non-governmental organizations (NGOs) are intensively involved in the excavation of Singapore's heritage for public viewing. This ongoing spectacle is in all ways haunted by the official scripted version of Singapore's national history often referred to as "The Singapore Story"; a story of the rise of the nation state based on the 1998 memoirs of Lee Kuan Yew, Singapore's first prime minister who governed for three decades. Blackburn (2013) outlines the emergence of heritage projects in

Singapore, official and populist. Singapore's National Heritage Board formed in 1993, and describes itself as the "custodian of Singapore's heritage."[65] The Board formed under the Ministry of Culture, Community, and Youth manages museums, heritage interpretative centers, institutions, and precincts.

Blackburn (2013) reflects upon the "democratization" of state-sponsored heritage projects that include the National Library's Singapore Memory Project and the National Archives of Singapore's oral history project, which have generated similar projects, many of which are web-based sites where Singaporeans can post their memories of Singapore's past as heritage. In 1987, the Singapore Heritage Society was established as an "independent voice for heritage conservation in Singapore."[66] The interest in "the living presence of the past" has led Singaporeans to not only upload personal memories on state-sponsored and private websites, but has also led to heritage activism with the formation of groups to identify, and in many cases preserve local places, cultural practices, buildings and so forth for heritage purposes. For example, during the years this fieldwork took place, a Chinese cemetery designated for removal known as Bukit Brown became a significant site for heritage activism by a group of Singaporeans who came together to prevent its destruction. Finally, Blackburn notes the increase of blogs, Facebook pages, YouTube channels and other web-based sites where Singaporeans construct heritage.

Lily Kong (1999), interested in the manner in which "different constructions of heritage converge or diverge," critically examined the official invention of "a popular music heritage" in 1990s Singapore. Kong notes these official inventions of heritage sanitize Singapore's popular music past of "undesirable" elements – drugs and rock and roll – constructing "partial reclamation" projects which situate the swinging sixties at a "safe distance" from the moral panic of the time (ibid., p. 12). Kong examined an archive of oral history material collected by the National Archives of Singapore in preparation for a 1996 exhibition – Retrospin – which focused on Singapore music. She noted that the recordings "revealed a palpable sense of heritage... comprising the raw material of common identity and belonging" (ibid., p. 14). It is this sense of heritage that Kong argues is "largely unsung" in official heritage projects focusing on Singapore's music history (ibid., p. 6). While the National Heritage Board recognizes such sources referred to as "intangible cultural heritage (ICH)," that is, heritage embodied in the bearers themselves, the Singaporean rockers of the 1960s remain mostly unrecognized by state-sponsored heritage projects.

Heritage, and what I refer to here as vernacular heritage, cannot be so easily conceptualized along this institutional classificatory framework. In the case of the small community of musicians, fans, friends, and family at the heart of this book, and any other sonic sojourners for that matter, the distinction between

Figure 37. An example of maintaining a safe distance from the 1960s. Photo by author, 2017.

tangible and intangible heritage does not exist – instead it is the convergence of human and non-human forces, things and thoughts, sensibilities and sentimental action assembled in emergent networks of intangible and tangible heritage materials that make up the vernacular heritage generated at any one time, in any one place. For this small community of musicians, heritage – embodied in Kiang but also in guitars, amplifiers, songs, riffs, jams, performances, alcohol use, talking cock, hanging out together – is the glue that binds us together in spite of our varying backgrounds, age, gender, class, and ethnicity. This social assembled as vernacular heritage is at the very heart of the Singaporean cosmopolitanism celebrated by this group of people. "Heritage" is often generated as a hegemonic, highly institutionalized project of commemoration that is productive of collective identities – most often in the function of nation-building.[67] "Working-class heritage" has been characterized as counter to the "shared past of the nation" of institutions and regulations that was set in place as part of the state's bureaucracy to administer its significant, distinctive past and the national cultural objects deemed worthy of preservation (Smith, Shackle, and Campbell 2011). Vernacular heritage in this case thrives on egalitarianism: any status is emergent and associated with either music making or arranging for making music. While a guitarist during jam sessions, performances, and so forth may be able to "distinguish" themselves through skill and talent, great care is taken to protect the egalitarian cosmopolitan nature of the community. Professors, shipping-container brokers, advertising consultants, the unemployed, and aging can all find a place, if they just show up. Showing up is an important key that signals the manifest frame of reciprocity communicating potential obligations that maintain the enduring quality emergent with each assemblage, each instance of community.

The "extent to which different constructions of heritage converge or diverge" is in part determined by the presence of built forms and cityscape characteristics central to the production of sonic social life (Kong 1999: 1). From local bar to performance hall, from shopping mall basement to practice space, from Singapore to Ho Chi Minh City, different combinations of convergence and divergence appear. Heritage then has scale-ability similar to the spatio-sonic scales that shape the doings of music making. From bodies to performance halls, the convergences and divergences that Kong is interested in are assembled with varying constructions of heritage. The heritage effect among community members results in a social reflexivity emergent in the assemblages of vernacular heritage that not only binds this music community together, but reminds all involved of the value of making distinctions between "popular morality and official morality" in terms of Singapore's national and social histories that network these urban places and their many associations (Thompson 1993).

Vernacular heritage making provides participants with a subject position to work with vis-a-vis the Singaporean state and its story. Kiang and associates construct a vernacular heritage within a "community of interest" organized around rebellious behavior and "cosmopolitan conviviality." The "palpable sense of heritage" Kong identifies is the one I encountered, historically anchored in a locally rich Southeast Asian sonic cosmopolitanism.

Heritage Straydogs Style

Figure 38. Heritage, The Straydogs way. Photo by author, 2012.

Guitar 77, the guitar shop where I first met Kiang and the others, posted on its website the following description of this veteran rocker:

> Kiang (aka Dennis or Old Man, sometimes Dirty Old Man) is no stranger to the local music scene. He is the 'hot' bassist of recently

revived 70's rockers, Stray Dogs...yes he is that old! Needless to say he is musically influenced by all the 60's and 70's rock giants in particular Pink Floyd, The Beatles, Led Zeppelin and The Who. He is also a huge fan of local Alternative Funk Rock band, Ugly In The Morning, and can frequently be seen at their shows scaring some of the other fans with his cheering and screeching like a drunken little girl (UITM loves him for this!). Besides teaching himself how to play the guitar and the bass, Old Man learned to play the Conga and the Cajon under the tutelage of Faiser Florez.[68]

The 1960s and '70s, participants' age, classic rock bands and their music, Singaporean locality, and drunken lewd behavior are strung together, forming the elements of vernacular heritage that counter state-sponsored versions of national heritage. Intimately tied together, the two versions refer to each other as each emerges in context. Kiang's credentials are further enhanced by membership of a legendary band and the fact that, like most rock musicians from those days, he taught himself to play music and become a "hot bassist" on the local music scene. This network of ability, things, sonic similitudes, bands, gear and persons stands in stark contrast to the professional music scene in Singapore. Talent levels, ability to read music, and range of repertoire differentiate the professional music community from a musical community of interest rooted deeply in vernacular heritage. It must be remembered that the community described in this book is made up of amateur musicians who have day jobs and rarely are paid for their performances.

I became aware of Kiang's aura of "intangible cultural heritage" simply by hanging out in his guitar shop on weekends after I arrived to Singapore in 2011. Sitting at the counter, sipping Kopi-O, I met many friends and fans who came to see "Uncle," to acquire advice regarding guitar gear, reminisce about the old days, and to check out what was new to the shop's inventory. During these encounters I learned of the extent of his fame and infamy as an embodiment of the 1960s rock scene in this Southeast Asian crossroads. These encounters introduced me to the "palpable sense of heritage... comprising the raw material of common identity and belonging" that Kong (1999) refers to. I would return to the university library to search for scholarship and archival materials that address this period and aspect of Singaporean history, and then return to the shop on weekends to discuss with Kiang, James, and others what I had discovered.

Kiang is fiercely loyal to the performance of rocker masculinity. James, on the other hand, having become a successful businessman, engages lightly with this way of being a man, specifically in rehearsals, jam sessions, and musical performances. Kiang remains in character at all times, producing some awkward moments. The guitar shops draw many families with children shopping for musical instruments. I discovered that Singaporean youth to a great degree are introduced to guitars, drums, and so forth through their participations in church worship bands. Christianity has an overwhelming presence in Singapore, especially for Chinese Singaporeans. Mega-churches and evangelical congregations have become increasingly popular in contemporary Singapore. The worship band is a key element in these forms of Christian worship and has become a central encounter with a genre of rock music for youth in which the electric guitar, bass, and drum kit act as non-human forces in the production of this sociality. In spite of the deeply conservative religious conduct associated with families and their children who traffic Kiang's guitar shop, the alcohol consumption and coarse language did not disappear. Maintaining the rocker persona, sometimes described as Kiang's "business model," at times had the effect of driving potential customers away from his shop. This business model effect was especially evident during happy hour jam sessions, as alcohol consumption was visibly present, and talking cock amplified masculine performances and experiences. The response of others was not always negative. Some customers enjoyed the revelry, and some simply ignored the goings on while they shopped. Moreover, Kiang and the rest of us knew there were some limits to the publicly displayed sensuous conduct, controlling our language and rocker rebelliousness when appropriate and necessary.

Inappropriate behavior in public settings, however, reveals another important aspect of the intangible heritage Kiang and the rocker mentality embody: the fact that we all make mistakes. In the Singaporean context in which getting ahead is strongly encouraged in a meritocracy that rewards perfection and excellence, making mistakes is disturbing for some Singaporeans. However, in Kiang's case, and for some others in the small community in which Kiang participates, making mistakes is central to the rocker lifestyle; a lifestyle counter to the conventional one promoted by the Singaporean state and its institutions. The school system at every level, the political system, and the representation and actuality of economic success strongly discourage and denigrate making mistakes. Kiang often confided in me that he enjoyed playing with me in a band because I didn't care about mistakes, particularly mistakes he made while rehearsing and performing. I replied that this is who we are: a group of old men, amateur musicians, prone to making mistakes. In fact, I suggested, and Kiang, James, and others agreed, musical mistakes are what make our music special, especially in Singapore. This feature of intangible cultural heritage does not stop at making music but extends into other private and public realms of existence and experience. For Blues 77, the band that Kiang, James, and I formed, the mistake is one of the performative elements that binds us together, establishing and maintaining our unique friendship and evoking empathic understandings of our limits and possibilities as friends, men, and musicians. In the social relations of vernacular heritage formed by this community of interest, it is the capacity and so the performativity of mistakes that are the terms of endearment. The suspension of the perception of the value of perfection and unending success, emergent with the celebration of the mistake, provides respite in a space of dependence discursively produced by the ever-present Singapore Story. In jam sessions, rehearsals, out-of-the-way corners of a basement shopping mall, and even in public performances, we can all be less than perfect, not quite able to achieve the ultimate success required of us.

The presence of such a band built upon the capacity for mistakes is highlighted in a musical landscape dominated by the performance of cover tunes in which the merits of performance are measured by the closeness to which the imitation matches the original. Pointed out in an earlier chapter, there is a certain amount of cultural cringe associated with the reproduction of English-language music. This extends to the musicality of "cover tunes" as well. Performing guitar solos as performed on original recordings, sounding "just like the album" are goals for many if not most bands in Singapore. Kiang and others in our community of musicians also play in a Pink Floyd tribute band. A current goal of this band is to perform the *Dark Side of the Moon* album exactly as it was recorded, complete with para-musical attributes (cash register sounds, and so forth). Musical mistakes, and original music, are not so welcomed in a musical soundscape dominated by familiar music that audiences refer to through comparisons to the original.

Whether appreciated or not, making mistakes and, in our case playing original music – sonic features of The Straydogs – creates attributes of the intangible cultural heritage around which this group of musicians thrive. If "Old Man" gets too drunk to perform, or I forget the lyrics, or James messes up on endings and beginnings, it does not matter; these are expected outcomes of old rockers who taught themselves how to play their instruments, and continue to perform in spite of many limitations, especially in light of our advancing age. In this way intangible cultural heritage counters national expectations of efficiency, progress, perfection, and unlimited success. Mistakes are the very essence of Kong's notion of "palpable sense of heritage… comprising the raw material of common identity and belonging." Making mistakes in music and life converge as heritage.

From Vernacular to National Heritage and Back Again

Our first performance as Blues 77 at the old Hood Bar & Café on Keong Saik Road in Chinatown was a performance of vernacular heritage. One of The Straydogs early guitarists was returning from Cornwall, England, to Singapore for a visit. Jimmy Appadurai is a legendary Singaporean guitarist who performed with The Straydogs and the Meltones in 1960s Singapore (see Figure 17). Clement, owner of Hood, arranged to have us and other blues bands perform in honor of his return. Jimmy joined us on stage for an all-out blues jam to end the evening's performances. This was the first public appearance of Blues 77.

Figure 39. Jamming vernacular heritage at Hood. Photo by Mitch Aso, 2012.

What became clear to me that evening was a community rooted in structural time – a generation of Singaporeans who had grown up and grown old over the course of history that began with independence and extended into contemporary times. Talk of the 1960s music scene filled the air. Hugs and cheers all around continued throughout the evening until levels of intoxication and esprit de corps reached fever pitch. The entire evening was one large talking cock session as Kiang shouted from the stage when we began: "We're talking cock." It was this performance and this night that I realized that my hobby was becoming something else: perhaps a project. It was this performance and this night that I realized I was learning something about Singapore and its history that was different from the typical. These "atypical Singaporeans" were in the midst of telling stories to themselves about themselves that countered the Singapore Story as told by the state. State-sponsored forms of pragmatic, rational economic behavior, the foundation of a Singaporean identity fostered by state narratives were being disassembled by irrational modes of conspicuous consumption and gifting. Deep sound and deep intoxication converged within the walls of Hood as sonics that reached ear-splitting levels of amplification. The rebellious rocker, a star that appeared during the 1960s days of yellow culture, emerged as a star once again. As bands performed, a sonic vernacular heritage, as tangible as could be, emerged in a cultural construction of reality recognizable to a generation of Chinese Singaporean men and women that was clearly memorable indeed.

Of course these are "modes of cultural consumption" at odds with those proffered by the state as productive and appropriate, and as contributing to the Singaporean national story. While intense and exuberant consumption of food and alcohol, especially when attending live music events in bars, is a common pattern among Singaporean men in general, excessive and eruptive behavior is hardly appropriate heritage material for official projects. As Kong (1999) notes this "unsung heritage" in Singapore remains so for "particular ideological reasons." For state purposes it is risky to engage in the production of innocently ciphered images of this hidden history in the Singaporean story, especially for the kinds of performance venues that assemble state spectacles around longstanding national themes of multiculturalism, productive citizenship, progressive economic management, and, of course, heritage that support these foundations in the Singapore Story.

The lifestyle of brawls, drinks, and women that was the target of national fear when The Straydogs were performing in the 1960s and '70s, continues to have social potential in spite of several decades of official silencing of rock and roll in the name of nation-building. In fact, Kiang and his bandmates in the past and present are fiercely proud Singaporeans complete with all the chauvinisms often associated with such local affinity. Guitar 77 and the networks actuated in the various places I have had the opportunity to be a part of, revealed the persistent presence of these "undesirable" elements in the ongoing emergence of vernacular heritage. Official heritage projects directed at the 1960s Singaporean music scene as Kong noted have kept these social and behavioral problems at a safe distance. By erasing their presence from the record, national heritage projects focus on the recognition of local content and talent that foster state ideologies of national pride and belonging (Kong 1999: 19). The clear projection of a clean and swinging Singaporean music scene in favor of a circulating cosmopolitanism of globally shared social movements and youth culture exchanges, which one could assemble socially in place is at odds with the yellow culture campaigns and moral panic of the times.

Since the 1990s, interest in the 1960s Singapore music scene has increased among Singaporeans and at times for various national heritage projects attempting to recapture the vibrancy of independence and early nation-building. As Kong (1999) noted, the Retrospin exhibit marked this emerging interest in this mostly "unsung" period of Singaporean history. It was during these years that oral histories were collected for the National Archives of Singapore from many of the performers, and Joe Pereira's first book was published based on interviews with bands that had held court at the Golden Venus nightclub. As the first decade of the 21st century ended, 1960s Singapore has been revitalized again in mostly sanitized forms by the nation state, or at least in spite of the nation state, as worthy of taking part in Singapore's national heritage and history.

Kiang is frequently recruited to participate in several networks of heritage building. One network in which he participates, assembles around stories and remembrances of the Tanjong Pagar Railway Station also referred to as the Singapore Railway Station. Located at Keppel Road, the former Tajong Pagar Railway Station was the southern terminus of the network operated by Keretapi Tanah Melayu (KTM), the main railway operator in Malaysia, until June 30, 2011 when the station ceased operations and was relocated to Woodlands Train Checkpoint. Kiang's father, The Chief, managed the hotel located in the station. From time to time, the television news station, Channel News Asia, the national newspaper, the *Straits Times*, and other news outlets call upon Kiang to recount the heyday of train travel between Singapore and Malaysia for which the station itself stands as monument and as tangible heritage waiting to be exploited for historical and commercial repurposing. During these news appearances Kiang is often called upon to perform a song, further indexing his intangible heritage as a 1960s musician. The stories I hear are about two young teens, James and Kiang, spending nights together in empty hotel rooms, seeing ghosts, ranting about cosmological forces in the world, getting drunk, and raving about girls and rock music. They are stories anchored in a locally assembled cosmopolitanism actualized during the heady days of rocky relations between Singapore and Malaysia – youthful imaginings of local spirits and international sonic circuits converge. In this thoroughly urban place, the sonics of rock music and youthful shenanigans that explore an emerging crossroads of modernity in this jewel of the east present a heritage which the Singaporean state has been intent upon displacing and erasing in favor of modern progress, economic success, and sober rationality.

On several occasions during the 1990s and more recently, Kiang has been called upon to reunite The Straydogs for heritage performances. At age 62, I am now the newest and youngest member of this legendary Singaporean rock band. Over the course of the life of this project in sonic ethnography, I have had the opportunity to participate in these performances of heritage made as hybrid projects of vernacular and national heritage in which sonics, songs, persons, and stages are assembled with some script in mind. The Straydogs' performance staged for The Esplanade's Concert series known as a "Date with Friends" described earlier provides an ethnographic example of ways in which the boundaries between national and vernacular, tangible and intangible heritage blur. The Esplanade is Singapore's premier concert hall and serves as a "national" stage as well as a stage for large-scale commercial entertainment. The concert series was developed to perform heritage work in celebration of Singapore's 50th anniversary as a nation state. The program that evening was meant to remember the historical contributions of the "swinging sixties" complete with public lectures scheduled in the afternoon prior to the concert.

Figure 40. Placard for "A Date with Friends" concert series featuring Kiang. Photo by the author 2015.

The MC for the show explains as he introduces our performance:

> In the good old days of the Golden Venus, one of the bands, one of
> those outstanding bands is a group that once was the pioneers of the
> R & B and especially the blues scene in Singapore. They used to pack
> them in. Especially the military forces, the British military forces who
> were serving here in Singapore, RAF Seletar, RAF Changi, British Far
> East Media and places like that, they would go to the Golden Venus
> just for their cup of tea. Their brand of music which this band really
> served it hot and really bold. Ladies and Gentlemen, please welcome
> The Straydogs.[69]

This introduction locates the band in a national heritage steeped in the
acoustemologies of post-colonialism, war, independence, and, of course, cups
of tea. The audience, several thousand mostly older Singaporeans, gray hair and
all, sang along with Vernon and Veronica. The songs – "Where the Boys Are,"
"Satisfaction," "My Boy Lollipop," "The Thrill to Love You" – brought the
audience back to the nightclub music scene in which Singaporean singers and
musicians played the parts of international stars like Cliff Richard, Elvis Presley,
Connie Francis, and others. The Straydogs occupied similar similitudes of
modern popular culture circulating this crossroads of the east. While Ray
Anthony of Fried Ice became the "Jimi Hendrix of Singapore," The Straydogs
were a difficult band to re-orient in this way. Occupying these sonic subject
positions globally available in the popular culture of Singapore felt heroic, as
Siva Choy remarked in an interview in Joe Pereira's book, *Legends of the Golden
Venus* (1999: 13). Nevertheless, as the MC announced, The Straydogs and the
other bands from the swinging, sexy 1960s were mostly serving someone else
their cup of tea.

The Straydogs' reputation led to suspicions on the part of the concert
promoters and producers. We had to supply the Media Board with our set list
and song lyrics before we were approved to play the show. The stage manager was
concerned that we would be unable to play our set list in the allotted time, and
asked us to revise it. We refused, and actually out of the three bands we were the
only band to deliver our set within the time allocated. The concert producer
continually visited our dressing room back stage to check up on us, worried that
we were drinking, smoking, or engaging in other prohibited behavior. We were,
in fact, drinking from our hidden whiskey bottles snuck in by Kiang.

All of the members of The Straydogs assembled for rehearsals a week prior
to the Esplanade show. For seven nights we rehearsed new and old songs at the
jam studio at West Coast Recreational Centre. Each night we ran through the
set list twice before retiring to the front room of the studio to drink and tell
stories. After several bottles of whiskey and retelling colorful memories of

teenage life in Katong, we headed to a nearby late night hawker center for mi goreng and tea alia. Over the fried noodles and ginger tea, the stories of youthful pasts continued. I have now participated in several of these reunions and they all follow the same pattern. While making music and rehearsing our set list is the main goal, it is the storytelling that takes center stage. Sonics infuse these speech events with the aural history of life as young people growing up in Singapore, and specifically in Katong. The making of this urban life in the present is done so by reassembling the associations among things, people, events, feelings, and sounds, in an urban geography that includes bakeries, beaches, homes, trees, automobiles, food, drink, and alcohol, to name a few of the cast of characters each story requires. Teenage boys gathering together on rooftops so they can spy on couples having sex through unshaded windows. Smoking next to the tree near Ah Pui's coffee shop. Brawls and fights over girls, or some other youthful offense in need of revenge. Betting on horses at the racetrack. Wandering from house to house in search of playmates. Hearing Bob Dylan's version of "Blowing in the Wind" (compared to Peter, Paul, and Mary's), the record that inspired the sound of The Straydogs. These and many other stories were told again and again as the whiskey flowed with the music.

Figure 41. National heritage. The Straydogs performing at the Esplanade Theatre. Photo by Jamie Gillen, 2015.

Planning sessions for our reunion concerts were held at the home of a wealthy boyhood friend. These planning sessions provided more opportunities for stories, drinking, and eating unusual food. These afternoon meetings included Jeffrey Low, the original rhythm guitarist for The Straydogs and current manager of the band. Jeffrey was the football writer for the *Straits Times* for many decades, having only recently retired. Jeffrey was a crucial lynchpin for these vernacular heritage events. In many ways his wealth of band lore and his access to national media provided opportunities for the band to enact vernacular heritage publicly. Jeffrey helped organize the concerts and tea dances as well as the rehearsals that preceded the shows. His story telling and treasure chest of band lore bonded the group in an esprit de corps that produced wonderful shows.

Figure 42. The planning group. Shek and Jeffrey (Straydogs manager), with Kiang, James, and the author after the December 2016 tea dance held at Hood Bar & Café.

The revival of the tea dances was our shining achievement as cultural producers of vernacular heritage. While the Esplanade concert reflected a national interest in Singapore's music history, the tea dances held at Hood Bar & Café in December 2016 and March 2017 brought vernacular heritage (intangible and tangible) together with national heritage, resulting in the kind of convergences and divergences that Kong (1999) noted. On a Sunday afternoon in December 2016, hundreds of Singaporeans arrived at Hood Bar & Café to celebrate the 50th anniversary of the band. Also on the bill was Pest Infested, another popular rock band from the 1960s Singapore music scene. Blues 77 also performed as a warm-up act.

The immense crowd was there to see and hear The Straydogs and Pest Infested. From 2 pm until 6 pm the crowd remained standing as the bands played. We made enough money selling tickets to pay for Ronnie's airfare from Australia and Jimmy's airfare from Cornwall, with funds left over to pay Pest Infested for their performance, and for numerous bottles of good whiskey. Pest Infested performed classic rock covers, while we played a mix of our original hits and covers that appeared on The Straydogs' set lists back in the day. The planning sessions and rehearsals paid off, just as they had with the Esplanade concert. We were tight, and performed our set without many mistakes. The audience called out for our hits: "Cold Morning," "Freedom," "Mum's Too Pampering," and several audience members came to the stage to tell stories of their own youthful experiences of these songs and The Straydogs' music.

Hood Bar and Cafe
December 4, 2016 ⊘

Blues 77, Pest Infested and Straydogs rocking the house down!! What a legendary jam!!

Figure 43. Turnout for the 2015 tea dance at Hood.

The incredible turnout and success of the tea dance led to another in March 2017. It wasn't the money that inspired the repeat performance, this time with Ray Anthony (the Jimi Hendrix of Singapore) and his band Fried Ice. Rather, it was the experience generated that was the inspiration for a follow-up tea dance. The crowd was populated mostly by aging Singaporeans who had lived this sonic history. Kiang and the other band members were re-united with friends they had not seen in many decades. The same went for many in the crowd. In this way, structural time as a "social temporality" (Butler 1988: 520) produced for the audience and performers an emergent social reality for which heritage appeared as a "substance" in the experience and performance of a generational identity. This is the stuff of vernacular heritage made by the bearers of what the Singapore Heritage Society refers to as "intangible cultural heritage." The exuberance of this performativity did not go unnoticed. Makers of national heritage were in the crowd. The Straydogs and Pest Infested performed under the auspices of the National Arts Council in September 2017 at the School for Theatre and the Arts (SOTA). These convergences of vernacular, intangible, and national heritage point to the assembled, in-the-making quality of such projects anchored in networks of the social and in history. The divergences involved remain mostly hidden from view. Making history always involves compromise.

Considering the heritage projects described above it becomes difficult to disentangle national and vernacular, tangible and intangible features of "heritage" – each resounds in the other. The national uplifting of 1960s Singaporean vernacular heritage projects in the 21st century illustrates as with the use of urban space in Singapore intense relationships the dependencies involved: the state in the Esplanade performance provided the stage and attempted to control the engagements that took place with varying degrees of success. The tea dances, entirely organized at the local level, nevertheless, could only take place in an urban space zoned for food and beverage. The sonics of all of this, in spite of concern regarding the politics of the noise, are much more difficult to contain. The sounds of history and contemporary life in Singapore continue to resound in spite of many limitations to making sound. And in fact, the state revitalizations of its early history as heritage out of the rubble of yellow culture reveals this plasticity involved in heritage projects, and whether one can locate easily such projects in the classificatory system with distinctive features, objects, and practices.

Coda

Tiger, Horse, Dog

Figure 44. Friends: Kiang, James, and the author. Photo by Jeffrey Low, 2015.

The coda in music affords opportunities to look back on sonic proceedings while at the same time providing an outro – a sonic way out. From those first afternoons in the basement of the Peninsula Shopping Centre and onto Southeast Asian stages and music venues of all kinds, I experienced and have tried to illustrate in these pages the acoustemology of a group of mostly older Singaporean men, many of whom were successful musicians in the 1960s and 1970s. In this 21st century, Kiang, James, and the others continue a music-centered sociability, performing music in a context increasingly informed by the rise of "music heritage" in Singapore. In perhaps what appears as a series of adhocracies, the main themes explored in this book, forged from work as an ethnographer, and as a participant, begin with encountering the presence in Singapore of a cosmopolitan conviviality enacted as a moral economy mostly among men. The collection of music stores and guitar shops in the basement of a shopping mall affords opportunities for men and things, human and non-human forces, to assemble again and again; for this particular network organized in part around a legend, this social life fosters forms of cultural production and consumption often at odds with the values and norms celebrated in Lee Kuan Yew's Singapore Story. The counternarratives that inhere in both word and deed are articulated in urban places and as urban life. The Doghouse is an urban consequence of devotion to a way of knowing one's world to which sound and sonic life are central. Lived histories of urban places converge with the cultural productions of vernacular heritage that are crucial to the life of this group of musicians, friends, family, and fans. Musical genres, skills, and performances collide and combine into devices of saturation in which all involved can experience the life-force of the group – a life-force embodied in drinking, rebellion, and in English-language rock and roll. Ultimately, making noise is expressive, creative ground upon which these musicians, their friends, families, and fans live. Their noise – whether on stage or in the basement – signifies not only a judgment of taste, but operates as a sign of resilience in an urban home that has experienced perhaps the most rapid and overwhelming instances of urbanization on our planet. The Singaporean cityscape is one constantly undergoing change. Like the tree in Katong, Kiang, James, and the others continue to stand.

For the most part the analytic for this book is a simple amalgam of Feld's (2014) ideas regarding acoustemologies and Latour's (2005) approach to networks, assemblages, and the social. The world of things and expressive forms (along with the humans) Latour describes in his ethnography of science labs is not much different from the world of things and expressive forms (along with the humans) in music stores, performance venues, and sonic life. Admittedly, in my hands, the analytic here is less attentive to structures of inequality – gender, class, ethnicity, religious affiliation – and the presence of these structures in the actions and words of the people. The egalitarian ethos did not disguise the intersectionality of these structural elements assembled in different configurations in different places and times. Nevertheless, my attentions remained mostly phenomenological and less critical than some might desire from an ethnographic work so obviously about gender, in this case masculinity, and the description of mostly homosocial worlds. Following in the lineage Butler (1988) helped forge, I did not begin with gender, and in this case, masculinity as a "substantial model of identity," rather, masculinity emerges as a "constituted social temporality" – "discontinuous [in]… the appearance of substance" (p. 520). My hope is that the analysis as it is can be added to other analyses of inequality as an ethnographic example of ways in which men manage such things in their daily and musical lives.

An unusual element involved with this research, at least an unusual element for me, was the activities associated with our performances, and of course the performances themselves. "Research creation" is increasingly recognized as a "mode of knowing" which integrates creative processes as an element of a project or study (Chapman and Sawchuk 2012: 5). What I am referring to here as sonic ethnography others would refer to as "performative ethnography" (de Garis 1999). Performativity as an analytical framework now has a deep history in anthropology and the social sciences. Recently, Mol (2002) and Law (2004) argued for conceptualizations of the social that do not envision it as "constructed" but as "enacted." Once again Butler's (1988: 519) phenomenological analysis of gender as "stylized repetition of acts" seems foundational to this recent work emphasizing the performative in social life. My own training included a large dose of Goffman (1959), Bauman (1977), Huizinga (1950), Conquergood (1989), Bauman and Briggs (1990), among others and so the idea that "life itself is a dramatically enacted thing" (Goffman 1959: 72) seems reasonable. But the performances, jams, and rehearsals afforded sonically social experiences emergent in the performances of expressive forms that embody and communicate the values shared by Kiang, James, and all the others. Huizinga notes (1950: 10 & 14) that in performance, not only is a "sense of order" an aesthetic goal – the genre, the song, the band – this sense of order is also the experience of this aesthetic in its "actualization" in the contexts of jams, rehearsals and performances that is of great delight. Making music together relies on simultaneously emergent models of and for the social described here that assemble musical genres, musical skills, moral economies, egalitarianism, cosmopolitan conviviality, heritage, urban living and the cityscape that localize sonic life as deep sound. The performances are opportunities to represent the values shared by these musicians and their associates.

This sonic ethnography of making rock music and urban life in Singapore is informed by this deep sound, not only for writing culture but musicking it as well. Our original compositions are meant to "represent" the experiences Kiang, James, myself and others shared over the life of this project. The music and lyrics of these compositions (for example "Shiok-Lah") are performed as sonifications of our lives as researchers, friends, and band members. We argue that as sonic ethnographies, the compositions immersed in the experiences of a local community reverberate some of the central values shared by those involved in this community: cosmopolitan urbanism, masculine camaraderie, acoustemology. The song writing, the jams, rehearsals, and performances, the guitar shop talking cock sessions, the conference talks and public lectures, but also the social media presence of our various bands, the uploading of recorded performances, and other mediated cultural productions associated with this ethnography and the lives of those involved represent the employment of multiple media in in the "emergent form of storytelling that which tap into the flow of content across media" (Jenkins 2003). For anthropological purposes (Walley 2015: 624) such "transmedia approaches provide diverse spaces for engagement... offering valuable opportunities for expanded dialogue." Whether transmediated or "multimodal" ethnography (Pink 2011), this storytelling across multiple media represents a "shared epistemic project" (Wally 2015: 633) assembled from diverse historical experiences and ontologies.

Moreover, the performance element, the "creation as research" (Chapman and Sawchuk 2012: 7) aspect of this project shaped the nature of the fieldwork in ways I had not experienced previously as an anthropologist. My earlier work dealt with the management of suffering resulting from a health condition I have never experienced myself. As research creation, the ethnographic experience and the social I have described intensified research relationships, with particular intensities drawn around establishing and maintaining citizenship animated by a moral economy of reciprocity, egalitarianism, and urban cosmopolitanism. Membership in the band, and particularly a performing band, amplify the duties, responsivities, and obligations aligned with the enactments this particular assemblage of the social. The ethics that deepen sound for Kiang, myself, and the others, are the same ethics involved as when the rattan broom sweeping the streets in a Javanese neighborhood sounds out social requirements for the arrival of another emergent social: the ethics of showing up, mutuality, relationality. All ethnographic research involves some balance of these. But in this case, the performative quality to this work intensified the ethical nature of my "participant experiences" (Pink 2009). As sound deepens, so can social relationships exposing both to the emotional and relational ups and downs that occur in any enduring social relationship: a fragile sense of order whose possible demise is always in its makings. Of course the benefits and pleasures can be great.

Late one evening after a Straydogs rehearsal James, Kiang, and I ventured over to the late night hawker center for some noodles and tea. James, our resident spiritual expert, an interest that as far as I can tell reaches deep into his life history, began to ruminate on Chinese astrology. "Tiger, horse, dog. That's us," said James. We didn't discuss the attributes of these totems, just merely noting that James is a dog, Kiang a tiger, and myself a horse. The presence of each and each in association was simply explanation enough. We had grown up listening and playing the same music, yet thousands of miles apart involved in quite different histories. Tiger, horse, dog – a conjuncture wrought from "gestures of similitude" (Ferguson 2002: 557) that we assumed back in the day were uniquely our own. In conjunction we found that our distinct teenage entries into "the politics of membership in the 'world society'" (ibid., p. 558) occurred at a crossroads. As band members, and as music makers, the ethnocentric cosmopolitanism that early on provided a medium through which we could communicate insights into each of our life stories opened up to a historically anchored, rich Southeast Asian cosmopolitanism. Kiang and my other friends here in Singapore reminded me that this island nation has always been at the center of cosmo-politics immersed in a kind of "planetary conviviality" (Mignolo 2000) – a conviviality for the cosmopolitan forged locally across vast global networks. In comparison to Feld's (2012) ethnography of jazz musicians in Ghana, the people I had met and was going to meet also ascribed fully to the cosmopolitan commitment; however, in this case their commitments were always and continue to be framed by an intense loyalty to Singaporean identity fraught as it is with ethnic politics and crossroads consequences. Paradoxically this loyalty, reaching high levels of chauvinism at times, is enacted by those whose lived experiences and histories have cast them as a marginal aesthetic footnote in the Singapore Story.

James' recognition of our astrological collectivity was some kind of mark of friendship, or at the very least our individual histories and experiences had found a social life of mutual affection and interpersonal bonds common to renditions of friendship. During my years of university training, establishing friendships in the course of fieldwork was generally portrayed as something to be avoided. Or friendships were considered to be merely an imagined relationship on the part of the anthropologist, imposing some ethnocentric construct upon relationships established during the course of fieldwork. In either case, such misunderstandings and delusionary expectations are considered more often than not to poison such fieldwork encounters, and so the need for avoidance. Crick (1989) questions whether it is appropriate to use the term friend when referring to fieldwork relationships. Handelman (1998) suggests that the use of the term friend to describe a fieldwork relationship is a problem of "projective typification" on the part of the anthropologist. Ridler (1996) goes even further remarking that the use of the term friend is a kind of "epistemological violence." As Ridler (ibid., p 243) sees it "to live a moment through the optic of research, with the ulterior motive of representation, is already, at the outset, to be committed to the construction of deeply interpreted, hence selective, experience," and constitutes a different social reality from the other. He continues:

> It appears that many anthropologists find or construct friendships in the field which are framed in terms of this kind of projective typification, or of emotional dependency, instrumentalization and forms of psychological boundarying which they contrast with the search for mutuality, compatibility, recreation, and openness conceived of as more typical of their relationships at home (Ridler 1996: 245).

Paine (1969: 511) characterizes "middle-class friendship" for western, industrialized societies as a relationship based on the "equivalency of exchange." Simmel (1950) also finds in friendship "degrees of discretion, of reciprocal revelation and concealment." Affectivity and instrumentality both of which are seen by those involved in the relationship to be in effect through reciprocal exchange appear to be significant features of friendships, whether between persons of similarity, or homophilic relations, or persons of difference, or heterophilic relations, and even among human and supernatural beings. In the anthropological enterprise, the friendships that develop during fieldwork are not much different from how friendships form from difference and operate in general. The potential for the ethnographer and interlocutors to form friendships, heterophilic ones for sure, for which inequalities and differing intentionalities are intensely present, also exist in other cultural and social contexts as well. As Narayan (1986) found in her ethnographic work among women in the Kangra Valley of northwest India, "friendship is a cultural construction" that in spite of differences in caste is built as homophilic bonds that emphasize shared similarities rather than focusing attention on the heterophilic bonds of complementary difference. The spirit of friendship, haunted by a politics entangled in affect and practice offers to those involved what Derrida (1988: 633) describes as "a kind of asymmetrical and heteronomical curvature of the social space." He links this curvature with a kind of "violence" that he believes "has insinuated itself into the origin of the most innocent experiences of friendship or justice" (ibid.). For tiger, horse, dog – Kiang, myself, and James, respectively – as band members, as ethnographic interlocutors, and as friends, innocence and violence are ever-present providing enriched opportunities to learn and be-in-the-world.

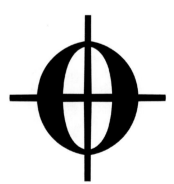

Figure 45. The coda.

So our friendships began with resemblances and led to understandings of our differences. Such is the nature of life at the crossroads. And it is interesting that the musical symbol for the coda is a continuous circling at a crossroads. Over the course of time, the affectivities and instrumentalities involved provided the contour to this making of our social space. Band membership rooted in rehearsal and performance is actualized reciprocally: reliance on each other to show up is at the very center of this form of play. The musicality is fostered sonically in the reciprocal exchanges that make up a song, whether performed or rehearsed. As Alfred Schutz (1964) once argued, "making music is making social relations," and in our case, sound, making music, sonic experience and history, gender and age conspire and in the process provide the social necessary for making friends. The extended music community – generational in some moments, multi-generational in others – made up of people, guitar gear, rehearsal studios, performance stages, bars, mall basements, emerges as a network of faith and motive: the very basis of friendship. My friendship with Kiang, James, and others I met along the way in Singapore reminds me at least, in its small way, that the content and livelihood of something large like globalization is embodied in human relationships, ultimately, and that humans affectively as well as instrumentally, make their worlds.

As I prepared to return home, I wrote a song that we rehearsed but have yet to perform.

"Can't Complain" (Ferzacca and Blues 77, 2017)
Verse and Chorus
Can't complain, can't complain about this life
Can't explain, can't explain this wild ride
It's luck you say, I must admit I'm mystified
Take every chance that comes your way
Cause you never know, listen to what I say
Don't be scared, you made it through yesterday
Its luck you say, I must admit I'm mystified
Take every chance that comes your way.
Bridge
Met up with some boys down in Singapore
Playing our guitars like never before
Rockin' in the basement till our spirits soar
It's not over yet, it's not over till we say so.[70]

Endnotes

1   https://youtu.be/oMDhBBtbAEE. Blues 77: Route 66 over Saigon. Published July 14, 2013.

2   For an informed history of The Straydogs available online, see https://m.facebook. com/notes/singapore-sixties-music/the-straydogs/134365316610971/. Accessed November 16, 2017. Joe Pereira's interview with Kiang, in his first book on the 1960s music scene in Singapore, *Legends of the Golden Venus* (Times Publishing, 1999, pp. 78–87), provides a history of the band as well.

3   https://youtu.be/H3gVR8P9zf0. Guitar 77: Steve and Kiang jam "Stormy Monday." Film by Sun Jung (1/2012). Published February 27, 2012.

4   There are many accounts of the Southeast Asian music scene in which playing popular music from Europe and the United States was the choice of many bands at the time. For example see: Lily Kong, 1999, 2006; Bart Barendregt, 2014; Joseph Pereira, 2011, 1999; Joseph Tham, 2014; Paul Augustin and James Lochhead, 2015.

5   See also Joseph Pereira, 2011. *Apache Over Singapore: The Story of Singapore Sixties Music*, Vol. 1. Select Publishing, pp: 148–152.

6   For detailed examinations of this music history in the region see Leiw 2016; Pereira 2011; Lockhard 1998.

7   Latour, 2005. Passages paraphrased from the "Introduction."

8   The ones that have informed my thinking and this project include but are not limited to: Bart Barendregt, *Sonic Modernities in the Malay World: A History of Popular Music, Social Distinction and Novel Lifestyles 1930s–2000s*. Brill Academic Publishing, 2014; Steven Feld. *Jazz Cosmopolitanism in Accra: Five Musical Years in Ghana*. Duke University Press, 2012; Charles K. Hirschkind, 2006. *The Ethical Soundscape: Cassette-Sermons and Islamic Counterpublics*. New York: Columbia University Press; Jacques Attali, 1995. *Noise: The Political Economy of Music*. Brian Massumi, trans. Minneapolis: University of Minnesota Press; Michael Bull and Les Back,eds., 2003. *The Auditory Culture Reader*. London: Berg; John Cage, 1961 Silence. Middletown, CT: Wesleyan University Press; Alain Corbin, 1998. *Village Bells: Sound and Meaning in the Nineteenth-Century French Countryside*. Martin Thom, trans. New York: Columbia University Press; Aaron Fox, 2004. *Real Country: Music, Language, Emotion and Sociability in Texas Working-Class Culture*. Durham, NC: Duke University Press; Ward Keeler, 1987. *Javanese Shadow Plays, Javanese Selves*. Princeton: Princeton University Press; Richard Rath, 2003. *How Early America Sounded*. Ithaca, NY: Cornell University Press; Marina Roseman, 1991. *Healing Sounds from the Malaysian*

Rainforest. Berkeley: University of California Press; Edward L. Schieffelin, 1976. *The Sorrow of the Lonely and the Burning of the Dancers.* New York: St. Martin's Press; Murray R. Schafer, 1977. *The Tuning of the World,* New York: Knopf. Reissued as *The Soundscape: Our Sonic Environment and the Tuning of the World,* 1994. Rochester, VT: Destiny Books; Mark M. Smith, 2001. *Listening to Nineteenth-Century America.* Chapel Hill: University of North Carolina Press; Paul Stoller, 1989. *The Taste of Ethnographic Things: The Senses in Anthropology.* Philadelphia: University of Pennsylvania Press; Emily Thompson, 2002. *The Soundscape of Modernity: Architectural Acoustics and the Culture of Listening in America, 1900–1933.* Cambridge, MA: MIT Press.

9 https://youtu.be/BxMsUHmeJyE. Blues 77, "Shiok-Lah", Hood, May 26, 2012.

10 https://youtu.be/YUJkq1nq5BA. Blues 77, "On the (Doghouse) Floor," Red Noodle, Singapore, 2016.

11 https://youtu.be/QFGgPeLI1Cg. Blues 77, "Haiyan," Red Noodle, Singapore, 2016.

12 https://youtu.be/AuJ7CZhuTX8. Blues 77, "I'm a Man," Red Noodle, Singapore, 2016.

13 https://youtu.be/_nSjP15oQAE. Blues 77, "Hey Now," Red Noodle, Singapore, 2016.

14 https://youtu.be/-e8LgJo57QY. Blues 77, "Yangon," Red Noodle, Singapore, 2016.

15 https://youtu.be/_cH1pFEWcAg. Blues 77, "You Stay," Red Noodle, Singapore, 2016.

16 https://youtu.be/NVa5AUERFjM. Blues 77, "Going Crazy," Red Noodle, Singapore, 2016.

17 https://youtu.be/2uPqZm4-a0U). Blues 77, "Hendrixing", Ho Chi Minh City, 2014.

18 "Tommy Johnson." David Evans. London: Studio Vista, 1971.

19 The sources on crossroads in Asia and elsewhere are scattered, mostly concentrated in scholarship on Europe and Christian traditions. Several resources I've consulted include in no particular order: DD Kosambi (1962); Dr Jacoba Hooykaas, 1955. "The Gateway on the Crossroads?" Bijdragen tot de Taal-, Land- en Volkenkunde, Deel 111, 4de Afl. pp. 413–415; "The Crossroads in Hoodoo Magic and The Ritual of Selling Yourself to the Devil," http://www.luckymojo.com/crossroads.html (accessed October 15, 2014); Kayagata-sati Sutta: Mindfulness Immersed in the Body translated from the Pali by Thanissaro Bhikkhu (1997), http://www.accesstoinsight.org/tipitaka/mn/mn.119.than.html (accessed October 15, 2014); year unknown, ぼた餅や辻の仏も春の風 (botamochi ya tsuji no hotoke mo haru no kaze), rice cake with bean paste, for the crossroads Buddha, spring breeze.

20 "The Sex Drive: fast, furious, fantastic." *Strait Times* September 24, 2011: A2.

21   I draw liberally here from James Donald (2011: 31), "Sounds Like Hell: Beyond Dystopian Noise," in *Noir Urbanisms: Dystopic Images of the Modern City*, pp. 31–52, Gyan Prakash, editor. Princeton, NJ: Princeton University Press.

22   http://remembersingapore.wordpress.com/2012/06/13/singapore-veteran-shopping-malls/. Accessed October 20, 2014.

23   http://www.stproperty.sg/articles-property/commercial/peninsula-plaza--bargain-city-at-your-fingertips/a/128557. Accessed October 20, 2014.

24   Ibid.

25   http://www.travelfish.org/blogs/singapore/2011/09/26/peninsula-plaza-singapores-little-burma/. Accessed October 20, 2014.

26   https://foursquare.com/v/peninsula-plaza/4b10c006f964a5205c7523e3.

27   https://www.facebook.com/pg/PeninsulaPlazaSingapore/reviews/?ref=page_internal.

28   Lee Kuan Yew 1950. "The Returned Student." Talk given to the Malayan Forum at Malaya Hall, London on January 28, 1950.

29   One of the earliest covers we used to rehearse with was Howlin Wolf's 1961 version of "Ain't Superstitious" (written by Willie Dixon). Here is an example of a performance of our particular assemblage of English-language, vocal resonances, time, gear, and the capacity of the gear in action to achieve the sonic experiences that brought us together and kept us together: https://youtu.be/nOJb_jd0HHk.

30   Steve Ferzacca, Joe Pereira, and Lim Kiang, "Going Down the Escalator to the Crossroads of Heritage, Community, and Music in Singapore." Asia Research Institute conference, "The Resilience of Vernacular Heritage in Asian Cities." National University of Singapore. Nov. 6, 2014.

31   http://moca mborainbow.blogspot.sg/. Accessed January 3, 2018.

32   See Chua Beng Huat, *Life is Not Complete without Shopping*, Singapore: Singapore University Press, 2003.

33   For complete lo hei celebration video see https://www.youtube.com/watch?v=9CiA4MdjtRU&list=UUDwKnqMO9YQT392GPwnxZCA. February 6, 2012.

34   Chandy, G. (2000, July 23). Do you Remember? *The New Paper*, p. 12. Retrieved from NewspaperSG.

35   See Aljunied, S. 2011. The "other" Muhammadiyah movement: Singapore 1958–2008. *Journal of Southeast Asian Studies*, 42(2), 281–302. doi:10.1017/S0022463411000051.

36   Rachel Chan, 10 things to know about the 60s. *Straits Times* (Singapore). May 14, 2015 Thursday.; SECTION: LIFE!; Life Music; SING50.

37   Debord, G. 1994. *The Society of the Spectacle*. (Translated by Donald Nicholson-Smith) New York: Zone Books.

38   Cox, 1998: p. 2.

39   Harvey, 1985. "This reminds us that the real problem lies with the private character of property rights and the power these rights confer to appropriate

not only the labor but also the collective products of others. Put another way, the problem is not the common per se, but the relations between those who produce or capture it at a variety of scales." P. 78.

40 See also: Heng, G., Devan, J. (1992) "State Fatherhood: The Politics of Nationalism, Sexuality and Race in Singapore," pp. 343–64. In Parker, A., Russo, M., Sommer, D., Yaeger, P. (eds) *Nationalisms and Sexualities.* New York: Routledge, and Y.Y. Teo, 2015. Differentiated Deservedness: Governance through Familialist Social Policies in Singapore, TRaNS: Trans-Regional and National Studies of Southeast Asia 3(1): 73–93.

41 Of course, I'm referring to Goffman and Clifford Geertz's use of this concept. For the bodily scale I am drawing upon Ara Wilson, 2011, Foreign Bodies and National Scales: Medical Tourism in Thailand Body & Society17(2&3): 121–137; Parr, H. (2002) "Medical Geography: Diagnosing the Body in Medical and Health Geography," *Progress in Human Geography* 26(2): 240–51. See also: Smith, N. (2004) "Scale Bending and the Fate of the National," pp. 192–212. In E. Sheppard and B. McMaster (eds) *Scale and Geographic Inquiry: Nature, Society, and Method.* Malden, MA: Wiley-Blackwell, and Marston, S.A. (2000) "The Social Construction of Scale'," Progress in *Human Geography* 24(2): 219–42.

42 Yang Xi Clement. Personal communication. February 11, 2015.

43 Yang Xi Clement. Personal communication. February 11, 2015.

44 Yang Xi Clement. Personal communication. February 10, 2015.

45 Not long after this conversation an article appeared in Singapore's national newspaper, *Straits Times*, entitled "Debate over future of Substation" (Tuesday, March 1, 2016: D5). The article outlined the "spirited debate" emerging over the future and identity of one of Singapore's "few independent art spaces." A fear was expressed that the new director would move Substation in a direction that would add to the "'dearth' of spaces available for live music, especially noisier events." Promoter, Shaiful Risan was quoted as saying, "The noisy people are part of society and they, too, need a playground."

46 This passage draws upon a paraphrasing of Igor Koptytoff's, 1986 essay, "The Cultural Biography of Things: Commoditization as Process," In *The Social Life of Things: Commodities in Cultural Perspective*, Arjun Appadurai (ed.), pp. 64–91. Cambridge: Cambridge University Press.

47 David Harvey, 1985. *The Urbanization of Capital.* Baltimore; John Hopkins University Press; Kevin Cox, 1998. *Spaces of Dependence, Spaces of Engagement and the Politics of Scale, or: Looking for Local Politics. Political Geography* 17(1): 1–23. Dennis R. Judd, 1998. *The Case of the Missing Scales: a Commentary on Cox. Political Geography* 17(1): 30.

48 Kelvin Low. 2014. "The Spatial Politics of Noise." International Sociological Association 18th World Congress, Yokohama, July 13–19; 2011. "Sensory Transgressions in Urbanity: Rights, Citizenship, and Sensorial Experiences." *Sensory Urbanisms Workshop.* FASS Cities Cluster, NUS, November 11. Jim

Sykes. 2014. "Towards a Malayan Indian Sonic Geography: Sound and Social Relations in Colonial Singapore." In *Transitions in Indian Music and Dance in the Colonial Indian Ocean, c. 1750–1950*. University of Pennsylvania, April 26–27, 2013. Singaporean Hinduism: Tamil Drumming, Ethics and Labor in the Air-Conditioned Nation (Society for Ethnomusicology conference, Nov.

49 *Straits Times*, "Debate over future of Substation" (Tuesday, March 1, 2016: D5).

50 See Steven Feld, 2012, Jazz Cosmopolitanism in Accra: Five Musical Years in Ghana. Duke University Press, 2012 for a similar discussion of the centrality of cosmopolitanism in music making and identity formations, in this case in Africa.

51 Troubling, as it is used here, is a liberal paraphrasing of Judith Butler's use of the concept in *Gender Trouble: Feminism and the Subversion of Identity*, Routledge, 2006[1990].

52 "Freedom," The Straydogs, EMI Records, 1971.

53 See also Joseph Tham, 2014. "A History of English-Language Popular Music." In *Singapore Soundscape: Musical Renaissance of a Global City*, Jun Zubillaga-Pow and Ho Chee Kong (Eds.), pp. 128–139, Singapore: National Library Board, p. 132.

54 See also Joseph Pereira, 2011. *Apache Over Singapore: The Story of Singapore Sixties Music*, Vol. 1. Select Publishing, pp. 148–152.

55 Lydia Fish, 1993. Songs of Americans in the Vietnam War. http://faculty.buffalostate.edu/fishlm/folksongs/americansongs.htm. Accessed January 28, 2016.

56 "A Date with Friends." Esplanade Concert Hall. November 6, 2015.

57 Facebook message, February 4, 2016 (Thu 8:36 pm).

58 World Travel and Tourism Council, 2014. The Impact of Visa Facilitation in ASEAN Member States January 2014. https://www.wttc.org/-/media/files/reports/policy%20research/impact_asean.pdf. Accessed January 21, 2016.

59 Crossley (1998) refers to "sensuous conduct," as an "ongoing motivational state that modifies, controls, and directs behavior moment to moment."

60 See Riyad Eid and Emrys Hughes, 2013. "Drivers and Barriers to Online Social Networks' Usage: The Case of Facebook." In *Transdisciplinary Marketing Concepts and Emergent Methods for Virtual Environments*. Hatem El-Gohary (Ed.). http://www.igi-global.com.libproxy1.nus.edu.sg/gateway/chapter/full-text-pdf/79340. Accessed February 5, 2016.

61 www.reverbnation.com/blues77

62 RFC; http://quancafesaigon.vn.

63 Christian G. Appy, 1993. *Working-Class War: American Combat Soldiers and Vietnam*. University of North Carolina Press, p. 238.

64 Pereira, 2011, pp. 148–152.

65 https://www.nhb.gov.sg/. Accessed April 19, 2017.

66 https://www.facebook.com/notes/singapore-heritage-society/about-the-singapore-heritage-society/1031971943517108. Accessed April 19, 2017.

67 See Laurajane Smith, Paul A. Shackle, and Gary Campbell, 2011, "Introduction: Class Still Matters." In *Heritage, Labour and the Working Classes*, pp. 1–16, Routledge.
68 http://www.guitar77.com/. Accessed February 23, 2014.
69 https://youtu.be/O6dx02SPLhM "Duke" with opening dialogue. November 6, 2015.
70 https://youtu.be/HxkOF1pYsH4 "Can't Complain" July 7, 2017.

Bibliography

Adil Johan, 2014. "Disquieting Degeneracy: Policing Malaysian and Singaporean Popular Music Culture from the Mid-1960s to Early 1970s." In *Sonic Modernities in the Malay World: A History of Popular Music, Social Distinction and Novel Lifestyles* (1930s–2000s), Bart Barendregt (ed.), pp: 135–161, Brill.

S. Aljunied, 2011. "The 'other' Muhammadiyah movement: Singapore 1958–2008." *Journal of Southeast Asian Studies*, 42(2), 281–302.

Christian G. Appy, 1993. *Working-Class War: American Combat Soldiers and Vietnam.* University of North Carolina Press.

Jacques Attali, 1995. *Noise: The Political Economy of Music.* Brian Massumi, trans. Minneapolis: University of Minnesota Press.

Paul Augustin and James Lochhead, 2015. *Just for the Love of It: Popular Music in Penang 1930s–1060s.* Strategic Information and Research Development Centre, Petaling Jaya, Malaysia.

Bart Barendregt, 2014. *Sonic Modernities in the Malay World: A History of Popular Music, Social Distinction and Novel Lifestyles 1930s–2000s.* Brill Academic Publishing.

Richard Bauman, 1977. *Verbal Art as Performance.* Long Grove, Illinois: Waveland Press Inc.

Richard Bauman and Charles L. Briggs, 1990. "Poetics and Performance as Critical Perspectives on Language and Social Life." *Annual Review of Anthropology* 19: 59–88.

William O. Beeman, "The Anthropology of Theater and Spectacle." *Annual Review of Anthropology* 22, 1993: 369–393.

Rakesh M. Bhatt, 2001. "World Englishes." *Annual Review of Anthropology* 2001 30(1), 527–550.

John J. Brandon, 2014. Economic Growth in ASEAN Drives Demand for Low-Cost Air Carriers (February 26). http://asiafoundation.org/in-asia/2014/02/26/economic-growth-in-asean-drives-demand-for-low-cost-air-carriers/. Accessed January 21, 2016.

Michael Bull and Les Back, eds., 2003. *The Auditory Culture Reader.* London: Berg.

Judith Butler, 1988. "Performative Acts and Gender Constitution: An Essay in Phenomenology and Feminist Theory." Theatre Journal, Vol. 40, No. 4 (Dec.), pp. 519–531.

Judith Butler, 2006[1990]. *Gender Trouble: Feminism and the Subversion of Identity.* Routledge.

John Cage, 1961. *Silence.* Middletown, CT: Wesleyan University Press.

Alejo Carpentier, 1949. On the Marvelous Real in America. In *Magical Realism: Theory, History, Community.* Edited with an Introduction by Lois Parkinson Zamora and Wendy B. Faris. Pp. 75–88. Durham & London; Duke University Press, 1995.

Rachel Chan, "10 things to know about the 60s." the *Straits Times* (Singapore). May 14, 2015 Thursday. SECTION: LIFE!; Life Music; SING50.

G. Chandy (2000, July 23). "Do you Remember?" *The New Paper*, p. 12. Retrieved from NewspaperSG.

Veron Cheong (September 28, 2008). "Singapore 60s", http://mocamborainbow.blogspot.sg/ (accessed: 15 March 2014).

Chua Beng Huat, 2003. *Life is Not Complete without Shopping,* Singapore: Singapore University Press.

Chua Beng Huat, 2012. *Structure, Audience and Soft Power in East Asian Pop Culture.* Hong Kong University Press.

William E. Connolly, 2013. "The 'New Materialism' and the Fragility of Things." Millennium: *Journal of International Studies* 4(3): 399–412.

_____, 1999. *Why I Am Not a Secularist.* Minneapolis, MN: University Of Minnesota Press.

Dwight Conquergood, 1989. "Poetics, Play, Process, and Power: The Performative Turn in Anthropology." *Text & Performance Quarterly*, 9(1): 82–89.

Ananda Kentish Coomaraswamy, 1977. *Coomaraswamy 2: Selected Papers Metaphysics.* Princeton: Princeton University Press.

Alain Corbin, 1998. *Village Bells: Sound and Meaning in the Nineteenth-Century French Countryside.* Martin Thom, trans. New York: Columbia University Press.

Kevin Cox, 1998. "Spaces of Dependence, Spaces of Engagement and the Politics of Scale, or: Looking for Local Politics." *Political Geography* 17(1): 1–23.

Tim Cresswell, 2011. "Mobilities I: Catching up". Progress in Human Geography 35 (4): 550–558.

Malcolm Crick, 1989. "Representation of International Tourism in the Social Sciences: Sun, Sex, Sights, Savings, and Servility." *Annual Review of Anthropology* 18: 307–400.

Nick Crossley, 1998. Emotion and Communicative Action: Habermas, Linguistic Philosophy and Existentialism. In *Emotions in Social Life: Critical Themes and Contemporary Issues.* G. Bendelow and S. J. Williams, eds., Pp. 16–38. London and New York: Routledge.

Michel de Certeau, 1984. *The Practice of Everyday Life.* Translated by Steven F. Rendall. University of California Press.

Laurence de Garis, 1999. "Experiments in pro-wrestling: Toward a performative and sensuous sport ethnography." *Sociology of Sport Journal* 16: 65–74.

G. Debord, 1994. *The Society of the Spectacle.* (Translated by Donald Nicholson-Smith) New York: Zone Books.

Jacques Derrida, 1988. "The politics of friendship." *Journal of Philosophy*, 85: 632–644.

Philippe Descola, 2010. "Cognition, Perception and Worlding." *Interdisciplinary Science Reviews*, 35: 3–4, 334–340.

James Donald, 2011. Sounds Like Hell: Beyond Dystopian Noise. In *Noir Urbanisms: Dystopic Images of the Modern City*, Gyan Prakash, editor, pp. 31–52. Princeton University Press.

W.E.B. Du Bois, 1903. *The Souls of Black Folk*. Chicago: A.C. McClurg & Co.

Michelle Duffy and Gordon R. Waitt, 2013. "Home Sounds: Experiential Practices and Performativities of Hearing and Listening." *Social and Cultural Geography*, 14 (4), 466–481. (p. 472).

Nick Easen, 2012. In Asia, a boom in low-cost flights (April 2). http://www.bbc.com/travel/story/20120402-low-cost-flights-in-asia-booms. Accessed January 21, 2016.

Riyad Eid and Emrys Hughes, 2013. Drivers and Barriers to Online Social Networks' Usage: The Case of Facebook. In *Transdisciplinary Marketing Concepts and Emergent Methods for Virtual Environments*. Hatem El-Gohary (Ed.). http://www.igi-global.com.libproxy1.nus.edu.sg/gateway/chapter/full-text-pdf/79340. Accessed 5 February 2016.

Frantz Fanon, 1968[1963] *The Wretched of the Earth*. Constance Farrington trans. Grove Press/Black Cat.

Steven Feld, 2012. *Jazz Cosmopolitanism in Accra: Five Musical Years in Ghana*. Duke University Press.

James G. Ferguson, 2002. "Of Mimicry and Membership: Africans and the New World Society." *Cultural Anthropology*, Vol. 17, No. 4 (Nov.): 551–569.

Steve Ferzacca, 2012. Deep Sound, Country Feeling: Kroncong Music in a Javanese Neighborhood. Asia Research Institute. Working Paper Series No. 180. National University of Singapore.

_____, 2006. "Learning to Listen: Kroncong Music in a Javanese Neighborhood." *The Senses and Society* 1(3): 331–358.

_____, 2001. *Healing the Modern in a Central Javanese City*. Carolina Academic Press.

Richard Florida, 2002. *The Rise of the Creative Class: And How It's Transforming Work, Leisure, Community and Everyday Life*. New York: Basic Books

Michel Foucault, 2007. *Security, Territory, Population. Lectures at the Collège de France 1977–1978*. Translated by Graham Burchell. Basingstoke, UK: Palgrave Macmillan.

Aaron Fox, 2004. *Real Country: Music, Language, Emotion and Sociability in Texas Working-Class Culture*. Durham, NC: Duke University Press.

Simon Frith, 1996. "Music and Identity." In *Questions of Cultural Identity*, S. Hall and P. DuGay (Eds.), London; Sage: 100–127.

Clifford Geertz, 1973. "Deep Play: Notes on the Balinese Cockfight." In *The Interpretation of Cultures*. Basic Books.

_____, 1960. *Religion in Java*. University of Chicago Press.

Erving Goffman, 1959. *The Presentation of Self in Everyday Life*. Anchor Books; Doubleday.

Patrick Guinness, 2009. *Kampung, Islam and State in Urban Java*. Singapore: NUS Press.

Don Handelman, 1998. *Models and Mirrors: Towards an Anthropology of Public Events*. Berghahn Books.

David Harvey, 2000. *Spaces of Hope*. University of California Press.

_____, 1985. *The Urbanization of Capital*. Baltimore; John Hopkins University Press.

Limin Hee, 2005, "Singapore's Orchard Road as Conduit: Between Nostalgia and Authenticity." *Traditional Dwellings and Settlements Review*, Vol. 17, No. 1 (FALL): 51–63.

G. Heng, and J. Devan, 1992. State Fatherhood: The Politics of Nationalism, Sexuality and Race in Singapore, In *Nationalisms and Sexualities* A. Parker, M. Russo, D. Sommer, P. Yaeger, P. (Eds), pp. 343–64, . New York: Routledge.

Gerald C. Hickey, 2002. *Window on a War: An Anthropologist in the Vietnam Conflict*. Texas Tech University Press.

Charles K. Hirschkind, 2006. *The Ethical Soundscape: Cassette-Sermons and Islamic Counterpublics*. New York: Columbia University Press.

Hong Lysa and Huang JianLi, 2008. *The Scripting of a National History: Singapore and Its Pasts*. Singapore: NUS Press.

Dr Jacoba Hooykaas, 1955. "The Gateway on the Crossroads?" Bijdragen tot de Taal-, Land- en Volkenkunde, Deel 111, 4de Afl. pp. 413–415.

J. Huizinga, 1950. *Homo Ludens: A Study of the Play-Element in Culture*. Boston: Beacon Press.

Dennis R. Judd, 1998. "The Case of the Missing Scales: a Commentary on Cox." *Political Geography* 17(1): 30.

Henry Jenkins, 2003. Transmedia Storytelling. MIT Technology Review. https://www.technologyreview.com/s/401760/transmedia-storytelling/. Accessed February 3, 2019.

Andrew F. Jones, 2001. *Yellow Music: Media Culture and Colonial Modernity in the Chinese Jazz Age*. Duke University Press.

Ward Keeler, 1987. *Javanese Shadow Plays, Javanese Selves*. Princeton: Princeton University Press.

Lily Kong, 1999. "The Invention of Heritage: Popular Music in Singapore." *Asian Studies Review* 23(1): 1–25.

_____, 2006. "Music and Moral Geographies: Construction of 'Nation' and Identity in Singapore." *GeoJournal* 65: 103–111.

Igor Koptytoff, 1986. "The Cultural Biography of Things: Commoditization as Process," In *The Social Life of Things: Commodities in Cultural Perspective*, Arjun Appadurai (ed.), pp. 64–91. Cambridge: Cambridge University Press.

Damodar Dharmanand Kosambi, 1962. *Myth and Reality*. Popular Prakashan PVT. LTD.

Braj B. Kachru, 1983. *The Indianization of English: the English language in India.* Delhi; New York: Oxford.

Arthur Kleinman, Y. Yan, J. Jing, T. Pan, S. Lee, E. Zhang, F. Wu, and J. Guo, 2011. *Deep China: The Moral Life of the Person. What Anthropology and Psychiatry Tell us about China Today.* Berkeley: University of California Press.

Eddie C. Y. Kuo, 1978. "Multilingualism and Mass Media Communications in Singapore." *Asian Survey*, 18(10), pp. 1067–1083.

Scott Laderman, 2009. *Tours of Vietnam: War, Travel Guides, and Memory.* Duke University Press.

George Lakoff and Mark Johnson, 1980. *Metaphors We Live By.* University of Chicago Press.

Bruno Latour, 2005, *Reassembling the Social: An Introduction to Actor-Network-Theory,* Oxford University Press.

John Law, 2004. *After Method: Mess in social science research.* London, UK: Routledge.

Lee Kuan Yew 1950. "The Returned Student." Talk given to the Malayan Forum at Malaya Hall, London on January 28, 1950.

Kai Khiun Liew, 2016. *Transnational Memory and Popular Culture in East and Southeast Asia: Amnesia, Nostalgia, Heritage.* Rowman & Littlefield International.

Craig Lockhard, 1998. *Dance of Life: Popular Music and Politics in Southeast Asia.* University of Hawai'i Press.

Kelvin Low, 2014. "The Spatial Politics of Noise." International Sociological Association 18th World Congress, Yokohama, July, 13–19.

_____, 2011. "Sensory Transgressions in Urbanity: Rights, Citizenship, and Sensorial Experiences." Sensory Urbanisms Workshop. FASS Cities Cluster, NUS, November 11.

Maureen Mahon, 2000. "The Visible Evidence of Cultural Producers." *Annual Review of Anthropology* 29, 467–492.

S. A. Marston, 2000. "The Social Construction of Scale," *Progress in Human Geography* 24(2): 219–42.

Yasser Mattar, 2009. "Popular cultural cringe: Language as signifier of authenticity and quality in the Singaporean popular music market." *Popular Music*, 28(2), 179–195.

Walter D. Mignolo, 2000. "The Many Faces of Cosmo-polis: Border Thinking and Critical Cosmopolitanism." *Public Culture* Fall 12(3): 721–748

Annemarie Mol, 2002. *The Body Multiple: Ontology in Medical Practice.* Durham, NC: Duke University Press.

Niels Mulder, 1994. *Individual and Society in Java: a Cultural Analysis.* Yogyakarta, Indonesia: Gadjah Mada University Press.

Jean-Luc Nancy, 2007. *Listening.* Translated by Charlotte Mandell. New York, Fordham University Press.

Kirin Narayan, 1986. "Birds on a branch: girlfriends and wedding songs in Kangra." *Ethos* 14(1): 47–75.

Jan Newberry, 2006. *Back Door Java: State Formation and the Domestic in Working Class Java.* Peterborough, Ontario: Broadview Press.

Laura Noslzlopy and Matthew Issac Cohen (Eds.), 2010. *Contemporary Southeast Asian Performance: Transnational Perspectives.* Cambridge Scholars Publishing.

Robert Paine, 1969. "In Search of Friendship: An Exploratory Analysis in "Middle-Class" Culture." *Man* 4(4) (December): 505–524.

Gary B. Palmer and William R. Jankowiak, 1996. "Performance and Imagination: Toward an Anthropology of the Spectacular and the Mundane." *Cultural Anthropology*, 11(2) (May): 225–258.

H. Parr, 2002. "Medical Geography: Diagnosing the Body in Medical and Health Geography," *Progress in Human Geography* 26(2): 240–51.

Giuseppina Pellegrino, 2012. *The Politics of Proximity.* London: Ashgate.

Joseph Pereira, 2011. *Apache Over Singapore: The Story of Singapore Sixties Music, Vol. 1.* Select Publishing.

_____, 1999. *Legends of the Golden Venus.* Times Publishing.

Phua Yue Keng Roy and Lily Kong, 1995. Exploring Local Cultures: The Construction and Evolution of Meaning and Identity in Katong. In *Portraits of Places: History, Community, and Identity in Singapore*, Brenda S. A. Yeoh and Lily Kong, eds., pp. 117–139, Times Editions.

Sarah Pink, 2011. "Multimodality, multisensoriality and ethnographic knowing: social semiotics and the phenomenology of perception." *Qualitative Research*, 11(3), 261–276.

_____, 2009. *Doing Sensory Ethnography.* London: Sage.

Michael Pickering and Tony Green, 1987. "Towards a Cartography of the Vernacular Milieu" In *Everyday Culture: Popular Song and the Vernacular Milieu,* Michael Pickering & Tony Green, eds., pp. 1–38. Open University Press.

S. Rajaratnam, 1972. "Singapore: Global City" address to Singapore Press Club February 6, reprinted in S. Rajaratnam, *The Prophetic and the Political* pp. 223–231.

Richard Rath, 2003. *How Early America Sounded.* Ithaca, NY: Cornell University Press.

Keith Ridler, 1996. If Not the Words: Shared Practical Activity and Friendship in Fieldwork, In *Things As They Are: New Directions in Phenomenological Anthropology*, edited with an introduction by Michael Jackson, pp. 238–58, Indiana University Press.

Marina Roseman, 1991. *Healing Sounds from the Malaysian Rainforest*, Berkeley: University of California Press.

Victor R. Savage, Brenda S. A. Yeoh, 2004. *Toponymics – A Study of Singapore Street Names.* Eastern University Press.

Murray R. Schafer, 1977. *The Tuning of the World*, New York: Knopf. Reissued as *The Soundscape: Our Sonic Environment and the Tuning of the World*, 1994. Rochester, VT: Destiny Books.

Edward L. Schieffelin, 1976. *The Sorrow of the Lonely and the Burning of the Dancers.* New York: St. Martin's Press.

Alfred Schutz, 1964. "Making Music Together: A Study in Social Relationship." In *Collected Papers: Studies in Social Theory*, pp. 159–78. The Hague: Martinus Nijhoff.

James C. Scott, 1977. *The Moral Economy of the Peasant: Rebellion and Subsistence in Southeast Asia*. Yale University Press.

Rodolfo C. Severino, 2006. *Southeast Asia in Search of an ASEAN Community: Insights from the Former ASEAN Secretary-General*. Singapore: ISEAS Publishing.

Mimi Sheller and John Urry, 2006. "The New Mobilities Paradigm." *Environment and Planning* A 38 (2): 207–226.

Sharon Siddique, 1989. Singaporean Identity. In *Management of Success*, Kernial Singh Sandhu and Paul Wheatley, eds., pp. Institute of Southeast Asian Studies.

George Simmel, 1950. *The sociology of Georg Simmel* (K. H. Wolff, Trans.). New York, NY: Free Press.

George Simmel, 2001 [1903]. "The Metropolis and Mental Life." In Spillman, Lynette. *Cultural Sociology*. New York: Wiley-Blackwell.

Milton Singer, 1972. *When a Great Tradition Modernizes*. London, Pall Mall.

Christopher Small, 1998. *Musicking: The Meaning of Performing and Listening*. Hanover, NH: University Press of New England.

Laurajane Smith, Paul A. Shackle, and Gary Campbell, 2011. "Introduction: Class Still Matters." In *Heritage, Labour and the Working Classes*, L. Smith, P. A. Shackle, G. Campbell, eds., pp. 1–16, Routledge.

Mark M. Smith, 2001. *Listening to Nineteenth-Century America*. Chapel Hill: University of North Carolina Press.

N. Smith, 2004. "Scale Bending and the Fate of the National," In *Scale and Geographic Inquiry: Nature, Society, and Method*. E. Sheppard and B. McMaster (eds) pp. 192–212, Malden, MA: Wiley-Blackwell.

Susan J. Smith, 2000. "Performing the (sound)world." Environment and Planning D: *Society and Space*, volume 18: 615–637.

Paul Stange, 1984. "The Logic of Rasa in Java." Indonesia 38: 113–134.

Paul Stoller, 1989. *The Taste of Ethnographic Things: The Senses in Anthropology*. Philadelphia: University of Pennsylvania Press.

Jim Sykes. 2015. "Towards a Malayan Indian Sonic Geography: Sound and Social Relations in Colonial Singapore". *Journal of Southeast Asian Studies* 46(3) October: 485–513.

Kenneth P. Tan, 2003. "Sexing Up Singapore". *International Journal of Cultural Studies*, 6(4), 403–423.

Peter K. W. Tan, Vincent B. Y. Ooi, and Andy K. L. Chiang, 2006. "World Englishes or English as a Lingua Franca? A View from the Perspective of Non-Anglo Englishes." In *English in the World: Global Rules, Global Roles*, Rani Rubdy & Mario Saraceni, eds., pp. 84–94, Bloomsbury.

Shawna Tang and Sharon Ee Ling Quah, 2018. "Heteronormativity and Sexuality Politics in Singapore: The Female-Headed Households of Divorced and Lesbian Mothers." *Journal of Sociology* 54(4): 647–664.

Michael Taussig, 1993. *Mimesis and Alterity: A Particular History of the Senses*. Routledge.

Timothy D. Taylor, 1997. *Global Pop: World Music, World Markets*. Routledge.

Teo You Yenn, 2018. *This is What Inequality Looks Like: Essays by Teo You Yenn*. Singapore: Ethos Books.

Joseph Tham, 2014. "A History of English-Language Popular Music." In *Singapore Soundscape: Musical Renaissance of a Global City*, Jun Zubillaga-Pow and Ho Chee Kong (Eds.), pp. 128–139, Singapore: National Library Board.

E. P. Thompson, 1993. Rough Music. In *Customs in Common: Studies in Traditional Popular Culture*, pp. 467–538. New York: The New York Press.

Emily Thompson, 2002. *The Soundscape of Modernity: Architectural Acoustics and the Culture of Listening in America, 1900–1933*. Cambridge, MA: MIT Press.

Jeremy Wallach, 2008. *Modern Noise, Fluid Genres: Popular Music in Indonesia 1997–2001*. University of Wisconsin Press.

Christine J. Walley, 2015. "Transmedia as experimental ethnography: The Exist Zero Project, deindustrialization, and the politics of nostalgia." American Ethnologist 42(4): 624–639.

Jasmine Wang and Simon Lee, 2014. Asia's Budget Airline Invasion (February 13). http://www.bloomberg.com/bw/articles/2014-02-13/asias-budget-airline-invasion-cathay-pacific-defends-hong-kong. Accessed January 21, 2016.

Barbara Watson-Andaya, 1997. "Historicizing 'Modernity' in Southeast Asia," *Journal of the Economic and Social History of the Orient* 40: 391–409.

Ara Wilson, 2011. "Foreign Bodies and National Scales: Medical Tourism in Thailand." *Body & Society* 17(2&3): 121–137.

World Travel and Tourism Council, 2014. The Impact of Visa Facilitation in ASEAN Member States January 2014. https://www.wttc.org/-/media/files/reports/policy%20research/impact_asean.pdf. Accessed January 21, 2016.

Yao Souchou. 2007. *Singapore: The State and the Culture of Excess*. Routledge.

Junjia Ye, 2016, "Spatialising the politics of coexistence: gui ju (规矩) in Singapore." *Transactions* 41: 91–103.

Index

lo hei for, 48
Chinese opera performances, 65
Chinese Singaporean masculinity, 71
Choy, Shiva, 42, 129
    social imaginary of heroic
        sonification, 42
Christianity, in Singapore, 123
city space, compartmentalization of, 62
class-based consciousness and
    practicalities, 13
Cliff Richard (English band), 8, 38, 40,
    43, 61
coconut stick broom, sound of, 16
coda in music, 135, 140
    symbol for, 141
code switching, between singing and
    speaking, 37
Coleman, George Drumgoole, 32
Coleman House, 32
community-based musicking,
    intra-sonics of, 13
community cleanliness, government
    dictum of, 15
community of interests, 44, 47, 70–1,
    82, 90, 93, 121–22, 124
community of music lovers, 31, 49
Conrad, Joseph, 32
Cornelius, Vernon (Cliff Richard of
    Singapore), 39, 61
cosmopolitan commitment, 4, 45–6,
    137
cosmopolitan conviviality, 4, 20, 24, 31,
    42, 44–5, 49, 58–60, 70, 90–1, 95,
    121, 136–7
cosmopolitanism
    at crossroads, 38–45
    Singaporean, 120
    sonic, 44
cosmopolitan urbanism, 137
cover tunes, musicality of, 62, 124
creative class, development of, 6
Crossroad Blues, 25
crossroads, 23–50

in Asian maritime trade network, 24
blues, rock, and cosmopolitanism at,
    38–45
British Empire's crossroads of the
    East, 42
in Chinese medical treatises, 24
cosmopolitanism and the Social, 24–6
counter and discovery, 26–31
English language at, 35–8
family deities and ancestors, 24
"foreign talent" attracted to, 26
guitar shops, 24
of modernity, 128
musical reference, 24
in Pali texts, 24
as places where "meritorious public
    works" can occur, 24
rock and blues musicians, 24
selective localizations at, 45–50
in sonic history and experience, 35–8
story of a Faustian bargain, 25
in Vedic literature, 24
cultural and social disintegration, 26
cultural appropriation, processes of, 18
cultural capital, development of, 9
cultural consumption, modes of, 40, 126
cultural diplomacy, 95
cultural modernity, 43
cultural production and consumption,
    136
cultural psychology, 13
customary consciousness, 49–50
Cyclones, The, 39

Dark Side of the Moon album, 124
deep sound, 14–18
    implications and consequences of, 16
    social fabric of kampung experience
        and, 17
    in social life, 16
    sonic ethnography of, 30, 137
    sound-meaning, 17

Singaporean masculinity, 69, 71, 75
Singaporean musicians, 37
   opportunities for, 39
   Singaporean bands, 37
   socializing with British and American
      soldiers, 40
Singaporean state, permit and zoning
   practices of, 66
Singapore Heritage Society, 118, 133
Singapore Management University, 82
Singapore multiculturalism, rationalizing
   of, 60
Singapore Railway Station, *see* Tanjong
   Pagar Railway Station
Singapore Story, The, 4, 9, 41, 49–50,
   117, 124, 126, 136, 139
singing English, style and sonics of, 37
Singlish (Singaporean English), 36–7
Small, Christopher, 13
"Smoke on the Water" music, 44
smoking state secrets, 73–6
social disciplining, against public sonics,
   65
social harmony, in community life, 15
social integration, aspects of, 12
sociality, forms of, 45
social life, 10, 16, 30, 136–7, 139
   of the Javanese, 12
   phonography of, 18
   in Singapore, 102
   sonic social life, 120
social popularity, 41–2
social relations, 10, 16, 20–1, 62, 66–7,
   72, 81, 84, 93, 106–7, 124, 138, 141
   and conduct, 93
   in kampung, 13–14
   network of, 4
social soundscapes, 19
social structure and praxis, audible
   dialogue of, 15
somaphore, 15
somaphoric organizations
   centrality of, 17

of everyday life, 18
of social life, 16
of society, 15
sonic circuits
   boys trips, 107–15
   infrastructures and mobilities, 103–7
   touring, 97–103
   visa facilitations, budget airlines and
      mediated connectivity, 102–6
sonic commensality, 45
sonic cosmopolitanism, 44, 49, 119
sonic cultural geography, 66
sonic democracy, 66, 83, 85
sonic ethnography, 4, 10, 18–21, 50,
   100, 126
   of deep sound, 30, 135
   degree of "participant-experience" of,
      19, 30
   of making rock music and urban life,
      137
   methods of, 19
sonic ethos, 4
sonic expressions, of social prowess and
   assemblages, 19, 93, 95
sonic geography, of Singapore, 66–7
   hierarchy of scales and, 67
sonic knowledges, 18
sonic politics, significance of, 65
sonic resonance, 44
sonic scales
   Albi, story of, 73–6
   of atypical Singaporeans, 85–6
   bodily scales, 69–73
   embedded scales, 69–73
   gender performances, 69–73
   home musicking and practice spaces,
      67–8
   scale-ability of, 76–85
   sonic geography, 66–7
   spatio-sonic scales, 65–6
   and urban life, 65–97
sonic seductions, 42
sonic social life, production of, 120